Economic Uplift Streams

Empowering Students Transcending Current Circumstance Limitations.

Demetrio Mojica

Table of Contents

1 Chapter 1: Understanding the Economic Landscape

Economic limitations aren't just about lacking money; they're a complex web of interconnected challenges that can significantly impact a young person's opportunities and overall well-being. We're talking about access to quality education, healthcare, nutritious food, safe housing, and even basic necessities like internet access – things that many of us take for granted. When these things are scarce, it creates a ripple effect that can hinder a student's ability to thrive. It's not just about not having the latest gadgets, it is much bigger.

For students, these limitations can manifest in various ways. Think about a student who has to work a part-time job to support their family. While work experience can be valuable, it can also take away from study time, extracurricular activities, and even just the chance to relax and recharge. This can lead to lower grades, increased stress, and a feeling of being constantly behind. Similarly, limited access to healthcare can mean that a student's health problems go untreated, leading to absences and decreased concentration in class. These challenges are not just academic, they are social. The pressure of economic hardship can strain relationships with family and friends, leading to feelings of isolation and loneliness.

Imagine Sarah, a bright and ambitious student from a low-income neighborhood. Sarah dreams of becoming a doctor, but she faces numerous obstacles. Her family struggles to make ends meet, so she has to work after school to help pay the bills. Her school is underfunded, lacking resources like up-to-date textbooks and advanced placement courses. She doesn't have access to the same extracurricular activities as students from wealthier districts, limiting her opportunities to build her resume and develop her interests. All this adds up to a mountain of disadvantages that Sarah has to overcome, but her resilience and determination keep her going. She understands that economic limitations are not just about money; they're about opportunities, access, and the ability to pursue her dreams.

The impact on students extends beyond the classroom and into their future. Students from disadvantaged backgrounds are less likely to attend college, and even if they do, they often face challenges paying for tuition, books, and living expenses. This can lead to high levels of student debt, which can burden them for years to come. Even after graduation, these students may face discrimination in the job market, making it harder to find well-paying jobs that allow them to escape the cycle of poverty.

Furthermore, economic limitations can impact a student's mental and emotional health. The stress of financial insecurity can lead to anxiety, depression, and a feeling of hopelessness. Students may feel ashamed or embarrassed about their financial situation, leading them to withdraw from social activities and isolate themselves from their peers. This can create a vicious cycle, where economic hardship leads to mental health problems, which in turn make it harder to succeed academically and professionally.

Understanding the systemic nature of these challenges is crucial. Economic limitations are not simply the result of individual choices or lack of effort. They are often the product of deeply entrenched social and economic inequalities. Factors like race, ethnicity, gender, and geographic location can all play a role in determining a student's access to resources and opportunities. Recognizing these systemic barriers is the first step towards creating a more equitable society where all students have the chance to reach their full potential.

It's important to understand the difference between being frugal and facing actual economic limitations. Frugality is a choice; it's about making conscious decisions to save money and live within your means. Economic limitations, on the other hand, are not a choice; they are a set of circumstances that restrict a person's access to essential resources and opportunities. A frugal person might choose to buy generic brands to save money, while a student facing economic limitations might not be able to afford groceries at all.

For educators and mentors, recognizing the signs of economic hardship is essential. Students facing these challenges may exhibit certain behaviors, such as coming to school hungry, wearing worn-out clothes, or lacking necessary school supplies. They may also be withdrawn, anxious, or have difficulty concentrating in class. By being aware of these signs, educators and mentors can provide support and connect students with resources that can help them overcome their challenges.

Overcoming economic limitations requires a multifaceted approach that addresses both individual needs and systemic barriers. This includes providing students with access to financial aid, scholarships, and grants, as well as resources like tutoring programs, mentoring programs, and mental health services. It also involves advocating for policies that promote economic equality, such as raising the minimum wage, increasing access to affordable housing, and investing in education. By working together, we can create a society where all students have the opportunity to thrive, regardless of their economic background.

Finally, empowering students to advocate for themselves and their communities is vital. We should encourage them to participate in civic engagement, to voice their concerns, and to demand change. By giving students a voice, we can help them become agents of change and create a more just and equitable world. Remember, understanding the economic landscape is not just about recognizing the challenges; it's about empowering students to overcome them and create a brighter future for themselves and their communities. That is why, by breaking down those barriers, we create a more inclusive and prosperous future for everyone, enabling our students to not only survive but thrive, regardless of their starting point.

1.1 Defining Economic Limitations

Economic limitations aren't just about a lack of money; they're about the barriers that prevent young people from reaching their full potential, it's about restricted opportunities that hinder growth, education, and future prospects. These limitations can manifest in various ways, impacting not only their financial well-being but also their mental and emotional health. Let's delve deeper into understanding these constraints.

Access to quality education, or rather, the lack thereof, is often the first and most significant hurdle. Students from disadvantaged backgrounds may attend underfunded schools with limited resources, from outdated textbooks to fewer extracurricular activities. This disparity creates a cycle where they are less prepared for higher education and future employment, perpetuating economic inequality. I remember a friend, Sarah, who struggled to keep up in her advanced placement classes because her school lacked the resources for proper tutoring. She worked twice as hard, but the playing field wasn't level, which affected her confidence and ultimately her college application choices. This situation is far too common and illustrates how systemic disadvantages can limit opportunities.

Beyond academics, consider the impact of basic needs not being met. Hunger, inadequate housing, and lack of access to healthcare can significantly affect a student's ability to focus on their studies. It's difficult to concentrate on algebra when you're worried about where your next meal is coming from, or if you have a safe place to sleep. Moreover, the stress of these circumstances can lead to mental health issues like anxiety and depression, further hindering their academic performance and overall well-being. This constant state of survival can drain their mental and emotional resources, leaving little energy for schoolwork or future planning.

The lack of exposure to different career paths is another key economic limitation. Students from affluent backgrounds often have access to internships, shadowing opportunities, and networking connections that open doors to various professions. In contrast, students facing economic hardship may have limited exposure to such opportunities, leading them to believe that certain careers are simply out of reach. They might not know anyone in those fields or have the resources to pursue them. I've seen countless bright young people, who felt pressured to choose immediate income over long-term career goals simply because they lacked the resources and information to explore other options.

Furthermore, financial literacy is often absent from the curriculum in under-resourced schools. Without this knowledge, students are ill-equipped to manage their finances responsibly, leading to debt and further economic hardship. Understanding concepts like budgeting, saving, and investing is crucial for building a secure financial future. It allows them to make informed decisions about their money and avoid common pitfalls. For instance, many young adults fall prey to predatory lending practices or credit card debt simply because they haven't been taught the basics of personal finance. This lack of knowledge can have long-lasting consequences, hindering their ability to build wealth and achieve financial independence.

The digital divide presents yet another barrier. Access to computers, reliable internet, and digital literacy skills are essential for success in today's world. Students without access to these resources are at a significant disadvantage when it comes to completing assignments, conducting research, and applying for jobs. The shift to online learning during the pandemic highlighted this disparity, leaving many students struggling to keep up. This lack of access limits their ability to participate fully in the educational system and prepares them for a workforce increasingly reliant on

technology.
Social capital, or the networks of relationships and connections an individual possesses, plays a vital role in economic mobility. Students from disadvantaged backgrounds often lack access to strong social networks that can provide mentorship, guidance, and opportunities. Networking with professionals in their desired fields can open doors to internships, job opportunities, and valuable career advice. Building these connections can be challenging without the resources or know-how to navigate social and professional environments. I remember when I was younger, I struggled to get an internship, and it was thanks to a neighbor that I was able to get the required skill to succeed and land the job.
It's important to acknowledge the psychological impact of economic limitations. Constantly facing financial hardship can lead to feelings of shame, hopelessness, and low self-esteem. These emotions can affect their motivation, academic performance, and overall outlook on life. It's crucial to provide support and resources to address these emotional challenges and help students develop resilience. Building their confidence and self-worth is essential for overcoming obstacles and achieving their goals.
Breaking free from these economic limitations requires a multifaceted approach. It involves providing access to quality education, meeting basic needs, increasing exposure to career opportunities, promoting financial literacy, bridging the digital divide,

and building strong support systems. By addressing these challenges head-on, we can create a more equitable society where all students have the opportunity to thrive.

Addressing this inequality is not only a moral imperative but also an economic one. Investing in the education and well-being of young people from disadvantaged backgrounds yields significant returns for society as a whole. It leads to a more skilled and productive workforce, reduces poverty and crime, and fosters a more just and equitable society. By empowering these students to reach their full potential, we can create a brighter future for everyone.

1.2 The Impact on Students

Economic limitations cast a long shadow over students' lives, influencing everything from academic performance to mental well-being. These limitations aren't just about a lack of pocket money; they represent a complex web of challenges that can significantly impede a student's ability to thrive, and it's important to recognize these nuances if we hope to create meaningful change. We must examine the far-reaching implications of economic hardship, acknowledging the subtle and overt ways it manifests in the lives of young people, and work for a society that supports them by giving them equal rights.

The most obvious impact is on access to resources. Students from economically disadvantaged backgrounds often lack the basic tools necessary for academic success. Textbooks, reliable internet access, a quiet study space – these are things many take for granted, but they can be significant barriers for others. Beyond the tangible resources, consider the less visible ones: the ability to afford extracurricular activities, tutoring services, or even just healthy meals that fuel concentration and learning. These disparities create an uneven playing field, putting students from poorer backgrounds at an immediate disadvantage, creating a widening gap over time.

Academic performance suffers directly. A student struggling to make ends meet, or worried about family finances, is unlikely to be able to focus fully on their studies. The stress and anxiety associated with poverty can lead to decreased concentration, lower grades, and a general disengagement from school. Absenteeism can also become a problem, as students may need to work part-time jobs to support their families, or may lack access to transportation or appropriate clothing for school. Moreover, the pressure to contribute financially to the household can force students to prioritize work over education, leading to a cycle of poverty that is difficult to break.

The effect on mental and emotional well-being cannot be overstated. Growing up in poverty can be incredibly stressful and traumatic. Students from low-income families are more likely to experience anxiety, depression, and other mental health issues. The constant worry about money, the lack of security, and the feeling of being different from their peers can take a heavy toll on their emotional well-being. This can manifest in various ways, from social withdrawal and isolation to behavioral problems and even substance abuse. Schools need to be aware of these challenges and provide access to mental health services and support systems for students in need.

Beyond the immediate challenges, economic limitations can also shape a student's future aspirations and opportunities. Students from disadvantaged backgrounds may have limited exposure to different career paths and may lack the social capital necessary to navigate the professional world. They may also be less likely to pursue higher education, due to financial constraints or a lack of encouragement. This can perpetuate a cycle of poverty, limiting their ability to improve their economic circumstances and achieve their full potential. To address this, schools and communities need to provide students with access to career counseling, mentoring programs, and other resources that can help them explore their options and develop the skills they need to succeed.

The impact extends to social dynamics and feelings of belonging. Students from low-income families may feel ostracized or ashamed because of their economic circumstances. They may be unable to participate in social activities with their peers, or may feel self-conscious about their clothes or possessions. This can lead to feelings of isolation, loneliness, and low self-esteem. Schools should strive to create a more inclusive and equitable environment where all students feel valued and respected, regardless of their economic background. This can involve implementing policies that reduce the stigma associated with poverty, providing financial assistance for school activities, and promoting a culture of empathy and understanding.

Addressing the impact of economic limitations requires a multifaceted approach. It's not enough to simply provide financial assistance; we need to address the root causes of poverty and create systemic changes that promote economic opportunity for all students. This includes investing in early childhood education, providing access to affordable healthcare and housing, and creating jobs that pay a living wage. It also requires addressing the social and emotional needs of students from disadvantaged backgrounds, providing them with the support and resources they need to overcome the challenges they face.

Ultimately, empowering students to transcend their circumstances requires a collective effort. Schools, families, communities, and policymakers all have a role to play in creating a more equitable and just society. By working together, we can create a world where all students have the opportunity to thrive, regardless of their economic background. It means challenging our own biases and assumptions, listening to the voices of those who are most affected, and advocating for policies that promote social and economic justice. It's not just about giving students a hand up; it's about creating a system where everyone has a fair chance to succeed. This is our task, and a future we should all want to believe in. It takes us all for it to work, and we should not let our youth grow up in environments where they think they are alone.

2 Chapter 2: Foundational Financial Literacy

Let's dive into the world of money. It's not just about having it; it's about understanding it, controlling it, and making it work for you. Many think financial literacy is only for the wealthy, but that couldn't be further from the truth. It's a crucial skill for everyone, especially when you're starting out, and it's the foundation for building a more secure future. This chapter will give you the tools to build that foundation, no matter where you're starting from.

Budgeting isn't about restriction, it's about empowerment. Forget the image of meticulously tracking every penny in a spreadsheet if that's not your style. Find a system that works for you. Start by figuring out your income, and if that's irregular or inconsistent, average it out over a few months. Then, track your expenses. There are countless budgeting apps available that can automatically categorize your spending, making the process significantly easier. Mint, YNAB (You Need a Budget), and Personal

Capital are just a few examples. If you prefer a more traditional approach, a simple notebook and pen will work just as well. The key is consistency. Track everything, even the small expenses like that daily coffee or snack, because they add up faster than you think. Once you have a clear picture of your income and expenses, you can start allocating your money effectively. Prioritize essential needs like housing, food, and transportation. Then, allocate funds for your wants, keeping in mind your financial goals. Aim to create a budget that allows you to save a portion of your income each month, even if it's a small amount. Remember that a budget is a living document; it should be flexible and adjusted as your circumstances change. Don't be afraid to experiment with different budgeting methods until you find one that fits your lifestyle.

Saving isn't about the amount; it's about the habit. Start small, even if it's just $5 or $10 a week. The important thing is to make saving a regular part of your routine. One effective strategy is to automate your savings. Set up a recurring transfer from your checking account to a savings account each payday. This way, you're saving money without even thinking about it. Consider opening a high-yield savings account. These accounts typically offer higher interest rates than traditional savings accounts, allowing your money to grow faster. Research different banks and credit unions to find the best rates and terms. Another useful technique is to set specific financial goals. Maybe you're saving for a new laptop, a down payment on a car, or a trip. Having a clear goal in mind can make saving more motivating and less daunting. Break down your larger goals into smaller, more manageable steps. For example, if you're saving for a $1,000 laptop, aim to save $100 a month for ten months. Celebrate your progress along the way. When you reach a milestone, reward yourself (in a way that doesn't derail your savings goals, of course!).

Debt can be a useful tool, but it can also be a trap. Understanding the different types of debt and how they work is essential. Credit cards are a common form of debt, and they can be convenient, but they often come with high interest rates. If you're using credit cards, pay off your balance in full each month to avoid interest charges. If you're carrying a balance, focus on paying down the cards with the highest interest rates first. This is known as the debt avalanche method. Another approach is the debt snowball method, where you focus on paying off the smallest debts first, regardless of interest rate. This can provide a sense of accomplishment and momentum as you tackle your debt. Student loans are another common type of debt, and they can be a significant burden for many students. Research different repayment options, such as income-driven repayment plans, which can adjust your monthly payments based on your income and family size. Consider consolidating your student loans to simplify your payments and potentially lower your interest rate. Avoid taking on more debt than you can comfortably afford to repay. Before making a purchase, ask yourself if you really need it or if it's just a want. Delay gratification and save up for larger purchases instead of putting them on a credit card. Build an emergency fund to cover unexpected expenses, which can help you avoid going into debt when faced with unforeseen circumstances.

Building a strong financial foundation is a journey, not a destination. It takes time, effort, and discipline. Don't get discouraged if you make mistakes along the way. Learn from your mistakes and keep moving forward. Seek out reliable sources of information and advice. Talk to a trusted mentor, financial advisor, or family member. There are also many online resources available, such as educational websites, personal finance blogs, and podcasts. Take advantage of these resources to expand your knowledge and improve your financial skills. Remember that financial literacy is a lifelong learning process. The more you learn about money, the better equipped you'll be to make sound financial decisions and achieve your goals. Your future self will thank you for it. By mastering budgeting, saving, and understanding debt, you're taking the first steps towards financial independence and building a brighter future. You've got this.

2.1 Budgeting Basics

Budgeting: it's not just about saying "no" to that new video game or the latest fashion trend. It's about making smart choices that let you say "yes" to your future. Think of it as your personal financial roadmap, guiding you toward your goals, whether that's college, a cool apartment, or even starting your own business one day. It might seem daunting, but trust me, mastering the basics now will pay off big time later. We're diving into practical strategies, not just theory, that you can start using today. This isn't about deprivation; it's about empowerment.

The first step is understanding where your money is currently going. Most people have no real idea. Grab a notebook, use a spreadsheet, or download a budgeting app – whichever works best for you. For one month, track every single penny. I mean every penny. That coffee you grabbed on the way to school? Write it down. That impulse purchase at the mall? Write it down. Don't judge yourself, just observe. At the end of the month, categorize your spending: food, transportation, entertainment, school supplies, etc. Seeing it all laid out in black and white (or color, if you're using an app!) can be a real eye-opener. I remember when I did this for the first time, I was shocked at how much I was spending on takeout coffee. It seemed like a small amount each day, but it added up to a huge chunk of change over the course of a month.

Now that you know where your money is going, it's time to create a plan. This is where the actual "budget" comes in. Start by listing your income. This could be from a part-time job, allowance, or even money you earn from chores. Then, list your essential expenses: things you absolutely need to survive, like food, transportation to school or work, and any necessary school supplies. Next, identify your non-essential expenses: things you want but don't necessarily need, like entertainment, eating out, and new clothes. A common budgeting method is the 50/30/20 rule. Fifty percent of your income goes toward needs, thirty percent toward wants, and twenty percent toward savings and debt repayment. However, as a young person, you might want to adjust this to prioritize saving as much as possible while your expenses are likely lower than they will be later in life. For example, you might try 40/30/30, putting 30% toward savings and investments. It is worth considering how much you are spending on your hobbies, sometimes you can even try and monetize them to make some extra income.

Next up, let's get into the nitty-gritty of setting realistic financial goals. Forget about vague aspirations like "becoming rich someday." Those dreams are fine, but not actionable. Instead, think about concrete, achievable targets. Do you want to save $500 for a new laptop? Or maybe put away $100 each month toward a future car? Break down big goals into smaller, manageable steps. This makes them feel less overwhelming and more attainable. Write down your goals and stick them somewhere you'll see them every day – your bedroom mirror, your locker, even the background on your phone. Visual reminders can be surprisingly powerful. Set a timeline for each goal. When do you want to achieve it? This will help you determine how much you need to save each week or month. Make your goals SMART: Specific, Measurable, Achievable, Relevant, and Time-bound. For example, instead of "save money," try "save $20 per week for the next six months to buy a new video game console."

Finding ways to save money can actually be kind of fun. Look for discounts wherever you can. Student IDs often unlock discounts at stores, movie theaters, and museums. Embrace the library. Borrow books, movies, and music instead of buying them. Learn to cook. Eating out is a huge budget-buster. Cooking at home is almost always cheaper and healthier. Pack your own lunch. Skip the expensive cafeteria food and bring a sandwich and snacks from home. Consider finding a more affordable hobby. Some hobbies, like collecting rare stamps or playing golf, can be incredibly expensive. Look for activities that are free or low-cost, like reading, hiking, or playing sports with friends. One thing I always recommend is to automate your savings. Set up a recurring transfer from your checking account to your savings account each month. Even a small amount can add up over time. Make it automatic so you don't even have to think about it.

It's inevitable – you're going to make mistakes. Everyone does. Don't beat yourself up over it. The key is to learn from them and get back on track. If you overspend one month, analyze where you went wrong and adjust your budget for the following month. Did you underestimate your entertainment expenses? Did you get hit with an unexpected bill? Identify the problem and make a plan to avoid it in the future. Don't be afraid to ask for help. Talk to a trusted adult – a parent, teacher, or school counselor. They can offer guidance and support. They might even have some money-saving tips you haven't thought of. Financial literacy is a lifelong journey. The more you learn now, the better equipped you'll be to make smart financial decisions in the future. Keep reading books and articles about personal finance. Attend workshops and seminars. Take online courses. The more you know, the more confident you'll be in managing your money. Remember, budgeting isn't about restricting yourself. It's about empowering yourself to achieve your dreams. It's about making conscious choices that align with your values and goals. It's about taking control of your financial future and building a life you love.

2.2 Saving Strategies

Saving money, particularly when resources are scarce, might feel like an impossible feat. You might think, "How can I save when I barely have enough to cover my essential needs?" The good news is, saving doesn't always mean setting aside large sums. It's about building a habit, starting small, and consistently making choices that prioritize your financial well-being, even if it's just a little bit at a time. The key is to make saving an automatic part of your routine, like brushing your teeth.

One of the first steps toward successful saving is understanding where your money goes. Many of us underestimate our daily spending habits, failing to realize the cumulative impact of small, seemingly insignificant expenses. This is where tracking your expenses becomes invaluable. Start by using a simple notebook, a spreadsheet on your computer, or a budgeting app on your phone to record every penny you spend for a month. Be honest and thorough; don't leave anything out, from your morning coffee to that impulse purchase you made online. At the end of the month, categorize your spending (e.g., food, transportation, entertainment, etc.) to identify your biggest expense categories. This process might reveal areas where you can easily cut back without significantly impacting your quality of life. For instance, perhaps you're spending a surprising amount on eating out when you could prepare meals at home for a fraction of the cost.

Once you have a clear picture of your spending habits, you can begin to create a budget that aligns with your financial goals. The 50/30/20 rule is a simple and effective budgeting framework that many people find helpful. It suggests allocating 50% of your income to needs (housing, food, transportation, utilities), 30% to wants (entertainment, dining out, hobbies), and 20% to savings and debt repayment. Of course, you can adjust these percentages to suit your individual circumstances and priorities. If you have significant debt, you might need to allocate a larger portion of your income to debt repayment, even if it means temporarily reducing your spending on wants. Similarly, if you have ambitious savings goals, such as saving for college or a down payment on a house, you might want to aim for a higher savings rate. The most important thing is to create a budget that is realistic, sustainable, and tailored to your specific needs and goals. Don't be afraid to adjust it as your circumstances change.

Beyond budgeting, you could explore ways to automate your savings. Automating your savings means setting up a system where a certain amount of money is automatically transferred from your checking account to your savings account each month. This is a powerful strategy because it takes the decision-making out of the equation. You don't have to remember to save, and you're less likely to spend the money if it's already in your savings account. Many banks offer the option to set up recurring transfers online or through their mobile app. You can also use a variety of budgeting apps to automate your savings and track your progress towards your financial goals. Start small, even if it's just $25 or $50 per month. Over time, you can gradually increase the amount you're saving as your income grows and you become more comfortable with the process. The key is to make saving an automatic and effortless part of your financial routine.

Another effective saving strategy is to take advantage of found money. Found money refers to unexpected income, such as a tax refund, a bonus at work, or a gift from a relative. Instead of spending this money on impulse purchases, commit to saving it.

You can deposit it directly into your savings account, use it to pay down debt, or invest it for the future. Similarly, when you receive a raise at work, resist the urge to increase your spending. Instead, allocate a portion of the raise to your savings goals. By treating found money as an opportunity to accelerate your savings progress, you can reach your financial goals faster and build a more secure financial future.

Furthermore, consider the power of mindful spending. Mindful spending is about being intentional and deliberate with your purchases, rather than acting on impulse. Before making a purchase, ask yourself if you really need the item, if you can afford it, and if it aligns with your values. Avoid emotional spending, which is often triggered by stress, boredom, or sadness. Wait at least 24 hours before making non-essential purchases, especially if they are expensive. This waiting period will give you time to consider whether you really want the item and whether it's the best use of your money. By practicing mindful spending, you can reduce impulse purchases, save money, and make more conscious choices about how you allocate your resources.

Finally, remember that saving is a marathon, not a sprint. There will be times when you face unexpected expenses or setbacks that derail your savings progress. Don't get discouraged. The most important thing is to stay focused on your goals, learn from your mistakes, and keep moving forward. Celebrate your successes along the way, no matter how small they may seem. Each dollar you save brings you closer to achieving your financial goals and building a more secure future. Embrace the journey, and trust that with consistent effort and discipline, you can achieve financial success, regardless of your current circumstances.

2.3 Understanding Debt

Debt. That single word can evoke a sense of dread, a feeling of being trapped. But understanding debt is the first step to managing it effectively and ultimately, using it as a tool, rather than letting it control you. For us young adults, navigating the world of credit cards, student loans, and potential future mortgages can feel overwhelming. However, with knowledge and a plan, you can approach debt with confidence.

Let's start with the basics: debt is simply money you owe to someone else. This could be a bank, a credit card company, the government (in the case of student loans), or even a friend or family member. The key to understanding debt lies in recognizing the difference between good debt and bad debt. Good debt is generally considered an investment in your future, something that will appreciate in value or generate income over time. Examples include student loans (which, ideally, lead to higher earning potential) and a mortgage (which allows you to own property). Bad debt, on the other hand, is typically used for consumables or depreciating assets. Credit card debt accumulated from impulse purchases, or loans for non-essential items, often fall into this category. While some debt can be a tool that can make you rich. Too much debt can cause high stress, mental health issues, and can stop you from pursuing opportunities because all your resources are tied to paying your debt.

One of the most common forms of debt for young adults is student loan debt. It's important to understand the terms of your student loans – the interest rate, the repayment schedule, and any options for deferment or income-based repayment. Interest rates can vary significantly, so it's crucial to shop around and compare offers before taking out a loan. Additionally, be aware of the difference between federal and private student loans. Federal loans typically offer more flexible repayment options and potential loan forgiveness programs. When the time comes to repay, explore all your options to find a plan that fits your budget. Many graduates are surprised by the actual monthly payment and length of time it takes to repay the loan. Don't be afraid to reach out to your loan servicer for guidance.

Credit cards can be a powerful tool for building credit and earning rewards, but they can also quickly lead to debt if not used responsibly. The key is to treat your credit card like a debit card – only spend what you can afford to pay back in full each month. Avoid carrying a balance, as high interest rates can quickly inflate your debt. If you're just starting out, consider a secured credit card, which requires a security deposit and can help you build credit gradually. Be mindful of annual fees and other charges associated with credit cards, and choose a card that aligns with your spending habits and financial goals. Compare interest rates and rewards programs.

Another crucial aspect of understanding debt is creating a budget. A budget allows you to track your income and expenses, identify areas where you can cut back, and allocate funds for debt repayment. There are numerous budgeting apps and tools available that can simplify the process. Experiment with different methods until you find one that works for you. A simple spreadsheet can be just as effective as a fancy app. The goal is to gain a clear picture of your financial situation and make informed decisions about your spending.

Beyond budgeting, consider strategies for accelerating your debt repayment. The debt snowball method involves paying off your smallest debts first, regardless of the interest rate, to build momentum and motivation. The debt avalanche method focuses on paying off the debts with the highest interest rates first, which can save you money in the long run. Choose the method that best suits your personality and financial situation. Even small extra payments can make a big difference over time. Another option is to consider debt consolidation, which involves combining multiple debts into a single loan with a lower interest rate. This can simplify your payments and potentially save you money.

Let's talk about the psychological side of debt. Debt can be a significant source of stress and anxiety, affecting your mental and physical health. It's important to acknowledge these feelings and develop coping mechanisms. Talking to a trusted friend, family member, or financial advisor can provide support and guidance. Avoidance is never the answer. Facing your debt head-on, creating a plan, and taking small steps towards repayment can empower you and reduce stress. Remember, you're not alone. Millions of people are dealing with debt, and there are resources available to help you navigate the challenges.

Finally, remember that building a healthy relationship with debt is a lifelong journey. It requires ongoing education, discipline, and a willingness to adapt your strategies as your financial situation evolves. Don't be afraid to seek professional advice from a financial advisor or credit counselor. They can provide personalized guidance and help you develop a plan to achieve your financial goals. Stay informed about current economic trends and interest rates. Continuously evaluate your spending habits and identify areas where you can improve. With knowledge, planning, and perseverance, you can take control of your debt and build a brighter financial future.

3 Chapter 3: Educational Investment Strategies

Embarking on your educational journey requires more than just enrolling in courses and attending lectures; it demands a strategic approach to funding and utilizing available resources. Scholarships and grants are not merely handouts, they represent investments in your potential, and securing them is a skill worth mastering. Think of it as unlocking free money to fuel your dreams, but like any investment, it requires research, planning, and diligent execution.

First, understand the landscape. The world of scholarships and grants is vast and varied, from small, local awards to prestigious national programs. Don't limit yourself to the well-known options; explore niche scholarships based on your background, interests, or field of study. Websites like Sallie Mae, Scholarship America, and Fastweb are excellent starting points, but remember to dig deeper. Look into organizations related to your intended profession, community foundations, and even your parents' employers. Each has its own eligibility criteria, deadlines, and application processes, so keep meticulous notes.

The application process is where many students falter. It's not enough to simply meet the minimum requirements; you need to stand out. Your application is your chance to tell your story, to showcase your passion, your accomplishments, and your aspirations. Start by crafting a compelling personal essay. This isn't just a summary of your resume; it's an opportunity to connect with the scholarship committee on a human level. Share your experiences, your challenges, and your goals in a way that resonates with them. Be authentic, be vulnerable, and be clear about how the scholarship will help you achieve your educational and career aspirations. Don't shy away from highlighting any economic limitations you have overcome; demonstrating resilience and determination can be incredibly powerful.

Then, focus on the details. Every scholarship application is different, so pay close attention to the specific requirements. Make sure you understand the essay prompts, the word limits, and the required supporting documents. Proofread everything carefully, and ask a teacher, counselor, or trusted adult to review your application before you submit it. Typos and grammatical errors can be a death knell, no matter how compelling your story. Gather your transcripts, letters of recommendation, and any other required materials well in advance of the deadline. Don't wait until the last minute to request letters of recommendation; give your recommenders plenty of time to write thoughtful and personalized letters that speak to your strengths and potential. Follow up with them politely to ensure they submit their letters on time. Many scholarships have strict deadlines, and late applications will not be considered, no matter how deserving you are.

Securing funding is one part of the equation; maximizing your educational resources is equally important. Remember that tuition is only one component of the overall cost of education. Textbooks, supplies, transportation, and living expenses can quickly add up. To minimize these costs, consider buying used textbooks, renting textbooks, or borrowing them from the library. Look for online resources and open educational resources (OER) that can supplement your learning. Take advantage of free tutoring programs, writing centers, and other academic support services offered by your school. These resources can help you improve your grades, stay on track, and avoid the need for expensive private tutoring.

Embrace technology. Numerous online learning platforms offer free or low-cost courses that can enhance your skills and knowledge. Platforms like Coursera, edX, and Khan Academy provide access to a wide range of subjects, from math and science to humanities and arts. These courses can be especially valuable if you're struggling in a particular subject or want to explore new areas of interest. Furthermore, look for scholarships specifically aimed at students taking online courses or pursuing online degrees. These scholarships can help offset the cost of online education and make it more accessible.

Your network can become a source of opportunity, so actively connect with professors, classmates, and alumni. Building relationships with your professors can lead to research opportunities, internships, and even job offers. Participate in class discussions, attend office hours, and ask questions. Show your professors that you're engaged and interested in learning. Your classmates can also be valuable resources. Form study groups, share notes, and support each other. Networking with alumni can provide insights into different career paths and help you connect with potential employers. Attend alumni events, join online alumni groups, and reach out to alumni who work in your field of interest. Don't be afraid to ask for advice or mentoring; most alumni are happy to help current students succeed.

Consider the long game. Think about your career goals and how your education can help you achieve them. Research different career paths, talk to professionals in your field of interest, and explore internship opportunities. Internships can provide valuable hands-on experience, help you develop valuable skills, and give you a competitive edge in the job market. They can also help you determine whether a particular career path is right for you. Look for paid internships whenever possible; they can help you offset your living expenses while gaining valuable work experience. If you can't find a paid internship, consider volunteering or shadowing a professional in your field of interest. Even unpaid experience can be valuable in building your resume and expanding your network.

Ultimately, educational investment is about more than just money; it's about investing in yourself. It's about believing in your potential, pursuing your dreams, and making the most of every opportunity that comes your way. By securing funding, maximizing resources, and building a strong support system, you can overcome economic limitations and achieve your educational and career goals. Remember that success is not a destination; it's a journey. There will be challenges along the way, but with perseverance, determination, and a strategic mindset, you can achieve anything you set your mind to. You have the power to transform your life and create a brighter future for yourself and your community. Embrace the challenge, seize the opportunities, and never stop learning.

3.1 Scholarships and Grants

Securing financial aid for education can feel like navigating a labyrinth, especially when you're already facing economic hurdles. However, scholarships and grants represent a tangible pathway to lessening the financial strain of pursuing your dreams. It's not just about finding free money; it's about understanding the landscape, knowing where to look, and presenting yourself as the most compelling candidate. This chapter dives into the strategies and resources you need to unlock these opportunities. The first, and possibly most critical, step involves understanding the types of scholarships and grants available. Scholarships are typically merit-based, awarded for academic excellence, athletic prowess, artistic talent, or community involvement. Grants, on the other hand, are often need-based, designed to assist students from low-income backgrounds. Federal Pell Grants, for instance, are a cornerstone of need-based aid, while scholarships from private organizations can focus on specific demographics, fields of study, or even hobbies. Knowing the difference will allow you to target your efforts effectively. Don't just blanket the internet with applications; focus on opportunities where you have a realistic chance of success. Research is your best friend here, and it goes beyond simply Googling "scholarships."

Delving deeper, it's crucial to tailor your applications to each specific opportunity. A generic essay simply won't cut it. Scholarship committees are looking for authenticity and a clear demonstration of how their funding will impact your life and your educational goals. Read the eligibility requirements and essay prompts carefully, and then craft a compelling narrative that showcases your strengths and aspirations. For instance, if a scholarship emphasizes leadership, highlight your experiences leading clubs, organizing community events, or mentoring younger students. Quantify your achievements whenever possible – "Increased club membership by 30%" is far more impactful than "Led the club." It's not just about what you did, but the impact you made.

Speaking of applications, let's talk about the Free Application for Federal Student Aid (FAFSA). This is the gateway to most federal and state financial aid, including Pell Grants, subsidized loans, and work-study programs. Completing the FAFSA accurately and on time is non-negotiable. Pay close attention to deadlines, gather all necessary financial documents (tax returns, bank statements), and don't hesitate to seek assistance from your school's financial aid office if you have questions. The FAFSA can seem daunting, but it's a crucial step in accessing the financial support you need. Missed deadlines can mean missed opportunities, and accuracy prevents delays or disqualification.

Beyond the FAFSA, explore institutional aid offered directly by colleges and universities. Many institutions have generous scholarship programs for incoming and continuing students. Visit the financial aid websites of the schools you're interested in and look for merit-based scholarships, need-based grants, and departmental awards. Often, you'll need to submit a separate application for institutional aid, so pay attention to deadlines and eligibility criteria. Don't assume that federal aid is the only option; institutional aid can significantly reduce the overall cost of attendance. Sometimes, these scholarships are automatically considered with your application, but it's always worth investigating further.

Moreover, think outside the box when searching for scholarship opportunities. Don't limit yourself to the big, national scholarships; explore smaller, local awards offered by community organizations, businesses, and foundations. These smaller scholarships may have fewer applicants, increasing your chances of success. Check with your high school guidance counselor, local library, and community centers for information on local scholarship programs. Even a small award can make a difference and demonstrate your commitment to education. I remember when I was applying for college, there was a local scholarship from the Rotary Club specifically for students interested in community service; focusing on my volunteer work really helped me stand out.

Now, let's talk about writing a compelling scholarship essay. This is your opportunity to tell your story, showcase your personality, and demonstrate why you deserve the scholarship. Start by brainstorming your experiences, accomplishments, and aspirations. Identify key themes that align with the scholarship's values and craft a narrative that highlights those themes. Be authentic, specific, and passionate. Avoid generic statements and clichés. Share a personal anecdote that illustrates your strengths and your commitment to your goals. Proofread your essay carefully for grammar and spelling errors, and ask a trusted teacher, counselor, or mentor to review it and provide feedback. A well-written essay can make all the difference.

Remember to continuously refine your application strategy.

Keep track of the scholarships you've applied for, the deadlines, and the results. Analyze your successes and failures to identify areas for improvement. If you're not getting the results you want, seek feedback from scholarship committees or writing centers. Don't be afraid to ask for help. Persistence and perseverance are key to navigating the scholarship landscape. It's a competitive process, but with a strategic approach and a compelling narrative, you can increase your chances of securing the funding you need to achieve your educational goals. The process can be arduous, but the rewards are well worth the effort.

Finally, don't underestimate the power of networking. Talk to your teachers, counselors, mentors, and family members about your scholarship search. They may have valuable insights, connections, or resources that you're not aware of. Attend college fairs, scholarship workshops, and information sessions to learn more about financial aid opportunities and connect with representatives from colleges and scholarship organizations. Networking can open doors and provide you with a competitive edge. You never know where your next scholarship opportunity might come from. A simple conversation could lead to a life-changing opportunity.

3.2 Maximizing Educational Resources

Let's dive into how you can squeeze every last drop of value out of the educational resources available to you. Many students, especially those facing economic hardships, often overlook the plethora of support systems and opportunities right under their noses. It's not about having endless funding, but about being incredibly resourceful and knowing where to look and how to ask for what you need. Consider this your treasure map to unlocking hidden educational gold.

First, become a library aficionado, and don't just think of libraries as quiet places filled with books (though they are that, too!). Libraries today are dynamic learning hubs. Many offer free access to online databases packed with research articles, e-books, and even streaming educational content. Librarians themselves are invaluable resources; they can guide you through research, help you find credible sources, and even provide one-on-one tutoring on specific topics. Explore your local library's website or visit in person to discover the workshops, classes, and digital resources they offer, many of which are free. For example, I once met a student who used the library's free access to online software tutorials to master a coding language, which landed her a well-paying internship. That kind of resourceful thinking can change your trajectory.

Tutoring and academic support services are essential too. Your school or college likely offers free tutoring services, writing centers, and academic advising. Don't wait until you're drowning in coursework to seek help; proactive engagement with these resources can prevent academic struggles before they even begin. Writing centers can provide feedback on your essays and research papers, helping you improve your writing skills and earn better grades. Academic advisors can help you navigate course selection, explore career options, and develop a personalized academic plan. These services are designed to support your academic success, so take advantage of them. In my experience, students who regularly utilize tutoring services often see a significant improvement in their grades and overall academic performance.

Furthermore, explore online learning platforms. The internet is awash with free and low-cost educational resources. Websites like Khan Academy, Coursera (audit option), and edX offer courses on a wide range of subjects, from math and science to humanities and arts. These platforms provide flexible learning options, allowing you to study at your own pace and on your own schedule. They can be particularly useful for supplementing your classroom learning, reviewing challenging concepts, or exploring new subjects that interest you. Look for courses taught by renowned professors and experts in their fields. Many of these platforms also offer financial aid or scholarships for students who cannot afford the full course fees. I found a course on advanced calculus, completely free, that truly enhanced my understanding.

Don't forget about leveraging your network. Talk to your teachers, professors, and classmates about your academic goals and challenges. They may be able to offer valuable advice, connect you with resources, or even form study groups. Building a strong network of peers and mentors can provide emotional support, academic guidance, and career opportunities. Attend office hours regularly to ask questions and get personalized feedback from your instructors. Participate in class discussions and engage with your classmates to deepen your understanding of the material. Networking is not just about collecting contacts; it's about building genuine relationships that can support your academic and professional growth. A friend of mine received a job offer solely through a professor recommending her based on consistent engagement in class.

Consider free workshops and community programs. Many community centers, non-profit organizations, and local businesses offer free workshops and programs on various topics, from financial literacy and job skills to art and music. These programs can provide valuable learning experiences and help you develop new skills that can enhance your academic and career prospects. Look for workshops that align with your interests and goals, and don't be afraid to try something new. These programs can also be a great way to meet new people and expand your network. I once attended a free workshop on public speaking that significantly improved my confidence and communication skills, and I am usually quite shy.

Another often-overlooked resource is alumni networks. If you are attending a college or university, tap into the alumni network for mentorship, career advice, and even job opportunities. Alumni are often willing to help current students and recent graduates, providing valuable insights and connections. Attend alumni events, join alumni groups on social media, and reach out to alumni who work in fields that interest you. Don't be afraid to ask for advice or guidance; most alumni are happy to share their experiences and offer support. Networking with alumni can open doors to internships, job opportunities, and career advancement. I know many young adults who have found mentors and connections thanks to their high school and college alumni associations.

Finally, learn to advocate for yourself. Don't be afraid to ask for help when you need it. Communicate your needs and challenges to your teachers, professors, advisors, and other support staff. They are there to help you succeed, but they can't do that if they don't know what you're struggling with. Be proactive in seeking out resources and support, and don't give up easily. Remember, your education is an investment in your future, and you deserve to have access to the resources you need to thrive. If you don't feel like you are receiving adequate support, speak up and advocate for yourself. Sometimes, all it takes is asking for what you need to get the assistance you deserve. So, get out there and start maximizing those educational resources! You have the power to transform your future. And remember, success isn't always about having everything handed to you; it's often about how creatively you use what you have.

4 Chapter 4: Entrepreneurial Mindset & Skills

Let's dive into the world of entrepreneurship, not as some distant dream, but as a tangible possibility, a skill set you can cultivate right now. We're talking about transforming ideas into action, turning problems into opportunities, and building something of your own – brick by brick. Forget the image of the lone genius in a garage; entrepreneurship is about collaboration, adaptation, and relentless problem-solving, all skills you can hone.

The first step is spotting the need. Instead of passively observing your surroundings, actively look for gaps. What are people complaining about? What services are lacking? Is there a way to improve an existing product or service? Maybe the local laundromat is always overcrowded, presenting an opportunity for a mobile laundry service catering to busy students. Perhaps the campus bookstore lacks affordable study materials, paving the way for a peer-to-peer textbook exchange platform. Look at your own life, your friends' lives, and your community, and consider where needs aren't being met. Brainstorming with friends can unlock ideas you'd never think of alone. Don't dismiss "small" ideas; many successful businesses started by solving a seemingly trivial problem. Critically, don't assume an idea is already being done; research is key. Validate your assumptions and see who your potential competitors are. If there are existing competitors, that doesn't necessarily mean the idea is bad. It just means you need to find a way to differentiate yourself, to offer something unique or better. This could be through lower prices, better customer service, a more convenient location, or a unique feature. The crucial thing is to have a deep understanding of the market and to constantly test and refine your approach, and even, if you have more than one idea, you can ask a small portion of people to test each one of your products.

Now, about that scary thing: the business plan. Think of it not as a daunting document, but as a roadmap, a tool to guide you on your journey. At its core, it's about answering these questions: What problem are you solving? Who are your customers? How will you reach them? How will you make money? What resources do you need? Don't overcomplicate it. Start with a simple one-page summary outlining your business idea, target market, competitive advantage, and financial projections. A lean canvas is a great tool for this. The key sections of a formal plan include an executive summary (a brief overview of your business), a company description (detailing your mission, vision, and values), a market analysis (identifying your target market and competition), a description of your product or service, a marketing and sales strategy, a management team overview, and financial projections (including startup costs, revenue forecasts, and profitability analysis). Remember, it's a living document, not set in stone. As you learn and grow, you'll need to revise and update your plan. One common mistake is to be overly optimistic about your sales projections. Be realistic and factor in potential challenges. It's better to underestimate and exceed expectations than to overestimate and fall short. Focus on demonstrable value creation and remember that a great idea poorly executed will fail, while an average idea well executed will often succeed.

Marketing can feel overwhelming. Don't worry, you don't need a massive budget to get started. Start small, be creative, and focus on reaching your target audience directly. Think about where your potential customers spend their time online and offline. Are they on social media? At community events? At school clubs? Utilize free marketing channels like social media, email marketing, and content marketing (creating valuable content that attracts and engages your target audience). Word-of-mouth marketing is incredibly powerful, so encourage your customers to spread the word about your business. Offer incentives for referrals and ask for testimonials. Consider partnering with other businesses or organizations to reach a wider audience. Remember, marketing is not about selling; it's about building relationships and providing value. Focus on creating content that educates, entertains, and inspires your target audience. Tell your story, be authentic, and show your passion for what you do. A good starting point is understanding the unique selling proposition (USP) of your business. What makes you different from the competition? Once you know your USP, you can use it to craft compelling marketing messages that resonate with your target audience. Embrace the power of storytelling; people connect with stories, not just products.

Networking isn't just about collecting business cards; it's about building genuine connections. Start with the people you already know – friends, family, classmates, professors. Attend industry events, workshops, and conferences. Join relevant online communities and forums. Don't be afraid to reach out to people you admire in your field and ask for advice. When you meet someone new, focus on listening and learning about their interests and needs. Offer help and support whenever possible. Be genuinely interested in others, and they will be more likely to be interested in you. Remember, networking is a two-way street. It's not just about what you can get from others; it's also about what you can offer them. Collaboration can amplify your impact and accelerate your growth. Partnering with other entrepreneurs can give you access to new markets, resources, and expertise. Look for opportunities to collaborate on projects, share resources, and cross-promote each other's businesses. Networking effectively is crucial because you never know where your next opportunity will come from, and the business world is largely built on who you know and what they know about you.

Finally, the numbers game. Managing finances for startups can be daunting, but it's crucial for survival. Start by tracking every penny that comes in and out of your business. Use simple accounting software or a spreadsheet to keep track of your income and expenses. Create a budget and stick to it as closely as possible. Separate your personal finances from your business finances to avoid confusion. Open a separate bank account for your business and use it exclusively for business transactions. Learn how to read financial statements, such as income statements, balance sheets, and cash flow statements. These statements will give you valuable insights into the financial health of your business. Seek advice from a financial advisor or accountant if you need help understanding your finances. Secure funding judiciously, and never commit more than you can reasonably repay. Consider bootstrapping your business (using your own savings or revenue to fund growth) before seeking external funding. External funding can be helpful, but it also comes with strings attached. Manage your cash flow carefully and ensure you have enough money to cover your expenses. Late payments can damage your credit score and make it difficult to secure funding in the future.

Understand your profit margins and price your products or services accordingly. Remember, revenue is vanity, profit is sanity, and cash flow is king. One of the biggest mistakes entrepreneurs make is not understanding their costs. Be sure to factor in all costs, including direct costs, indirect costs, and fixed costs. Remember that financial literacy is a lifelong journey, and the more you learn, the better equipped you'll be to manage your finances and achieve your goals.

4.1 Identifying Opportunities

Let's get to the heart of opportunity – recognizing it. Seeing possibilities where others see problems is the cornerstone of any successful venture, and it's a skill you can hone. The world is constantly changing, presenting new challenges and, consequently, new avenues for innovation and profit. But how do you train your mind to spot these openings, especially when you're starting from a place of limited resources? It begins with a shift in perspective, a conscious effort to look beyond the surface and identify unmet needs and inefficiencies in the systems around you. Don't think you need a revolutionary idea; even small improvements to existing products or services can translate into significant opportunities. Think local. What are the needs of your community? What problems do people face every day that you might be able to solve, even in a small way? Could you offer a service that's currently unavailable or improve the quality or convenience of an existing one? Perhaps you notice that elderly neighbors struggle with grocery shopping, or that local students need tutoring in specific subjects. These are all potential starting points. Remember, the best opportunities often arise from addressing real-world problems. The key is to observe, listen, and think creatively.

Beyond observing, actively seek information. Read local newspapers, community forums, and social media groups to understand the prevailing issues and concerns. Attend community events and engage in conversations with people from different backgrounds and perspectives. The more you expose yourself to diverse viewpoints, the better equipped you'll be to identify unmet needs and potential solutions. Don't be afraid to ask questions and challenge assumptions. Why is something done a certain way? Could it be done better, faster, or cheaper? By questioning the status quo, you open yourself up to new possibilities. Furthermore, research existing businesses and industries in your area. What are their strengths and weaknesses? Are there any gaps in the market that they're not addressing? Identifying these gaps can reveal valuable opportunities for new ventures. Use online tools like Google Trends or local business directories to gather data and analyze market trends. The more information you have, the better equipped you'll be to make informed decisions. Don't underestimate the power of simple market research, like surveying potential customers or conducting informal inter-

views. Understanding your target market's needs and preferences is crucial for developing a successful product or service.
Consider your own skills and passions. What are you good at? What do you enjoy doing? The intersection of your skills and interests can often reveal unique opportunities. If you're passionate about photography, perhaps you could offer photography services to local businesses or individuals. If you're skilled in web design, you could create websites for small businesses that don't have an online presence. The key is to leverage your existing strengths and interests to create value for others. Don't be afraid to experiment and try new things. Even if you don't succeed at first, you'll learn valuable lessons that can help you in the future. Embrace failure as a learning opportunity and don't let it discourage you from pursuing your goals. Remember that many successful entrepreneurs have faced setbacks and challenges along the way. The important thing is to persevere and continue learning and growing.

Another crucial aspect of identifying opportunities is to cultivate a network of contacts. Attend industry events, join professional organizations, and connect with people who have experience in your field of interest. Networking can provide valuable insights, advice, and mentorship. Don't be afraid to reach out to people you admire and ask for their guidance. Most people are happy to share their knowledge and experience with aspiring entrepreneurs. Building relationships with potential customers, suppliers, and investors is also essential for success. Networking can open doors to new opportunities and help you overcome challenges. It's not just about what you know, but also who you know.

Finally, think about scalability and sustainability. Can your business idea be scaled up to reach a wider audience? Is it environmentally sustainable? Is it socially responsible? These are important considerations that can impact the long-term viability of your venture. Consider the potential impact of your business on the community and the environment. Aim to create a business that not only generates profit but also contributes to the well-being of society. Sustainability is becoming increasingly important to consumers, so businesses that prioritize environmental and social responsibility are more likely to succeed in the long run. Remember, identifying opportunities is not a passive process. It requires active engagement, critical thinking, and a willingness to take risks. By cultivating these skills, you can unlock your entrepreneurial potential and create a brighter future for yourself and your community. Don't just dream it, see it, analyze it, and make it a reality.

4.2 Business Plan Essentials

Crafting a comprehensive business plan is not merely filling out templates, but rather, meticulously charting a course from aspiration to achievement. As an aspiring entrepreneur, especially

navigating limited resources, consider your business plan as your compass and map, guiding every decision and mitigating potential pitfalls. It is the first step towards getting funding and securing investors, as well as a blueprint for success in your venture.
The initial stage involves defining your business concept with laser-like clarity. What specific problem are you solving, and for whom? Your target market should not be "everyone," but a well-defined group with specific needs. Conduct thorough market research to understand their pain points, preferences, and buying habits. This involves not only online research but also talking to potential customers directly through surveys, interviews, or focus groups. Understand your competition, not just their products or services, but their strengths, weaknesses, and pricing strategies. Differentiate yourself by identifying a unique selling proposition (USP). What makes you stand out from the crowd? Is it superior quality, lower prices, exceptional customer service, or a novel approach to solving the problem? The more niche and specific you are, the easier it will be to reach your customers and the more likely you will be to succeed.
Next, delve into the operational aspects. Detail the day-to-day workings of your business. Where will it be located? What equipment or resources will you need? How will you produce your product or deliver your service? Consider the scalability of your operations. Can you easily ramp up production or service delivery to meet growing demand? If not, identify potential bot-

tlenecks and develop strategies to address them. Outline your management team and their roles. Even if you are a solo entrepreneur, consider identifying potential advisors or mentors who can provide guidance and support. A well-defined operational plan demonstrates that you have thought through the practicalities of running your business and are prepared for the challenges ahead.

Financial projections are the backbone of any solid business plan. Don't be intimidated by numbers; instead, see them as a language you can learn to communicate your vision effectively. Start with realistic sales forecasts based on your market research and pricing strategy. Then, project your expenses, including fixed costs (rent, utilities, salaries) and variable costs (materials, marketing). Create a cash flow statement that shows how much money you expect to come in and go out each month. This will help you identify potential cash flow problems and plan accordingly. Develop a profit and loss (P&L) statement that summarizes your revenues, expenses, and profits over a specific period. Finally, create a balance sheet that shows your assets (what you own), liabilities (what you owe), and equity (your net worth). Consider different financial scenarios, such as best-case, worst-case, and most-likely-case. This will demonstrate that you have considered the potential risks and are prepared to adapt to changing circumstances.

Marketing strategy should be outlined in detail. How will you reach your target market? What channels will you use to promote your product or service? Develop a marketing budget that is realistic and affordable. Consider low-cost marketing strategies, such as social media marketing, content marketing, and email marketing. Network with other businesses and organizations in your community to build relationships and generate leads. Track your marketing efforts to measure their effectiveness and make adjustments as needed. Don't be afraid to experiment with different marketing tactics until you find what works best for your business.

A crucial component of any business plan is identifying and mitigating potential risks. What are the biggest threats to your business? It could be anything from competition and economic downturns to changes in technology or regulations. For each risk, develop a contingency plan that outlines the steps you will take to minimize its impact. This shows potential investors that you are aware of the challenges you may face and are prepared to overcome them. Don't gloss over the risks; be honest and transparent about the potential pitfalls of your business.

Finally, make sure your business plan is well-written, professional, and easy to understand. Use clear and concise language, avoid jargon, and proofread carefully for errors. Include a table of contents, executive summary, and appendices with supporting documents. Remember, your business plan is a reflection of your business. A well-crafted business plan demonstrates your commitment, professionalism, and attention to detail. In the journey of economic upliftment, your business plan is not just a document; it's your roadmap to success.

4.3 Marketing Fundamentals

Marketing isn't some abstract concept reserved for big corporations with million-dollar budgets; it's fundamentally about connecting with people and showing them why your idea, product, or service solves a problem they have. It's about understanding your target audience, what they need, and how to communicate your value in a way that resonates with them. Many people starting out think marketing is synonymous with advertising, but it's so much more comprehensive than that. It encompasses everything from product development and pricing to customer service and brand building. It's the entire process of bringing your idea to market and fostering lasting relationships with your customers. Let's say you want to start a small business selling homemade baked goods. Your marketing strategy isn't just about putting up flyers or posting on social media. It starts with understanding who your ideal customer is: are you targeting busy parents who need quick and easy desserts, students craving late-night snacks, or health-conscious individuals looking for gluten-free options? Once you know your audience, you can tailor your products, pricing, and messaging to appeal specifically to them.

The very first thing you need to understand is the "marketing mix," often referred to as the "4 Ps": Product, Price, Place, and Promotion. Product, of course, refers to what you're offering. Does it meet a specific need or solve a problem for your target audience? What makes it unique or better than the competition? Price is equally critical. How much are people willing to pay for your product or service? Are you positioning yourself as a premium brand or a budget-friendly option? Place refers to where your product or service is available. Is it online, in a physical store, or both? How accessible is it to your target audience? Promotion encompasses all the ways you communicate with your target audience. This includes advertising, social media, public relations, and sales promotions. Mastering these elements is key for a successful business, even if it's just a side hustle. Understanding how these elements interact is crucial for creating a cohesive and effective marketing strategy. For instance, a high-end product requires a high price point and a distribution strategy that places it in exclusive locations. Conversely, a budget-friendly product needs a lower price and a distribution strategy that makes it easily accessible to the masses.

Next, let's tackle target audience identification. Don't try to be everything to everyone. Instead, focus on identifying a specific group of people who are most likely to be interested in your product or service. Consider demographics like age, gender, location, and income, but also delve deeper into their psychographics, such as their interests, values, and lifestyle. Where do they spend their time online? What are their pain points and aspirations? Understanding your target audience deeply allows you to craft marketing messages that speak directly to their needs and desires. Let's return to our homemade baked goods example. If your target audience is health-conscious individuals, you might focus on highlighting the use of natural ingredients, low sugar content, and gluten-free options. You might promote your products at local farmers' markets or health food stores and partner with fitness influencers to reach a wider audience.

Now, let's talk about building your brand. Your brand is more than just a logo or a color scheme. It's the overall perception people have of your business. It's about creating a consistent and compelling message that resonates with your target audience and differentiates you from the competition. Your brand should reflect your values, your personality, and your unique selling proposition. Think about brands you admire. What makes them stand out? What emotions do they evoke? Your brand should be authentic and true to who you are. You may want to consider your values, too. Are you promoting environmental awareness? Or perhaps social justice causes? Do you want your customers to associate your product with fun or luxury? These are just some questions to ask yourself when branding. You can communicate it through your website, social media profiles, and even the way you interact with customers. Every interaction is an opportunity

to reinforce your brand and build trust.
Finally, let's discuss digital marketing fundamentals. In today's digital age, having a strong online presence is essential. This includes having a website or online store, being active on social media, and using email marketing to connect with your customers. Your website should be user-friendly, visually appealing, and optimized for search engines. Make sure it's easy for people to find what they're looking for and make a purchase. Social media is a powerful tool for building brand awareness, engaging with your audience, and driving traffic to your website. Choose the platforms that are most relevant to your target audience and create content that is informative, entertaining, and engaging. Email marketing is a great way to stay in touch with your customers, promote new products or services, and offer exclusive deals. Building an email list allows you to directly communicate with people who have already expressed interest in your business. These are just some of the many strategies you can use. Your efforts in the realm of marketing, no matter which techniques you use, should revolve around a singular, easily digested, and relatable theme.

4.4 Networking & Collaboration

Networking and collaboration aren't just buzzwords thrown around in business meetings; they're the lifeblood of any successful endeavor, especially when you're trying to build something from the ground up. Think of it as building a bridge – you can't construct it alone. You need a team, resources, and shared expertise to make it strong and stable. In the context of economic uplift, networking becomes a deliberate and powerful act of connecting with individuals and groups who can offer support, guidance, and opportunities. It's about forging alliances that amplify your efforts and create pathways to resources you might not otherwise access.

The first thing to understand is that networking isn't just about collecting business cards. That's a common misconception. It's about building genuine relationships, offering value, and creating mutually beneficial connections. You need to consider what you can bring to the table as well. What skills do you possess? What are you passionate about? What problems can you solve for others? Being able to articulate your value proposition is critical in making meaningful connections. Start small, think about the people you already know, friends, family, teachers, and mentors. These existing connections are the easiest to cultivate because there's already a foundation of trust and familiarity.

Beyond your inner circle, consider joining relevant organizations and attending industry events. These could be student clubs, community workshops, local business meetups, or even online forums. The key is to find environments where you can interact with like-minded individuals and professionals in your field of interest. When you attend these events, don't just stand in the corner hoping someone will approach you. Be proactive! Introduce yourself, ask questions, and actively listen to what others have to say. Remember to follow up with the people you meet. A simple email or LinkedIn message expressing your interest in staying connected can go a long way in solidifying a new relationship. Don't be afraid of rejection. Not every connection will lead to a fruitful collaboration, and that's perfectly okay. The important thing is to keep putting yourself out there and learning from each experience.

Collaboration, on the other hand, takes networking a step further. It's about working together towards a shared goal, combining your strengths and resources to achieve something bigger than you could on your own. Look for opportunities to collaborate on projects, whether it's starting a business, organizing a community event, or developing a new product or service. When choosing collaborators, look for individuals who complement your skills and share your values. Diversity of thought and experience can lead to innovative solutions and prevent groupthink. Be clear about your expectations and responsibilities from the outset. This includes outlining roles, timelines, and how decisions will be made. Open communication is key to resolving conflicts and ensuring that everyone feels valued and heard.

Furthermore, think about creative ways to leverage your network for economic uplift. Could you partner with a local business to offer internships or apprenticeships to other students? Could you organize a crowdfunding campaign to support a community project? Could you start a mentorship program to guide younger students? These initiatives not only benefit others but also enhance your own skills and reputation. Moreover, collaboration extends beyond individuals to organizations and institutions. Look for partnerships between schools, businesses, and community groups that can provide resources and opportunities for students. For example, a local business might offer workshops on financial literacy, or a community organization might provide access to affordable housing. These partnerships can create a ripple effect, empowering students and their families to overcome economic limitations.

Remember, building a strong network and fostering meaningful collaborations takes time and effort. It's not something that happens overnight. But with persistence, a genuine desire to help others, and a willingness to learn, you can create a powerful engine for economic uplift, not just for yourself, but for your entire community. Now, let's dive into practical exercises. Start by identifying three people in your existing network who could potentially offer guidance or support in your area of interest. Reach out to them and schedule a brief conversation to learn more about their experiences and insights. Next, research local organizations or events that align with your goals and interests. Attend one of these events and make a conscious effort to connect with at least two new people. Finally, brainstorm a project or initiative that you could collaborate on with others in your network. This could be anything from starting a small business to organizing a community service project. Take the first step towards making this idea a reality by outlining a basic plan and reaching out to potential collaborators. By actively engaging in these activities, you'll begin to build a strong network and develop the skills necessary to collaborate effectively.

Finally, keep in mind that networking and collaboration are not just about receiving; they're also about giving back. As you grow and develop your own skills and resources, remember to pay it forward by mentoring others, sharing your knowledge, and creating opportunities for those who are coming up behind you. This cycle of giving and receiving is what truly builds a strong and resilient community. Don't be afraid to share your own story and experiences with others. Your journey, with its challenges and triumphs, can inspire and motivate others to pursue their own dreams. Remember, your story is a powerful tool that can create connections and foster a sense of community. By embracing networking and collaboration as a continuous process, you can create a powerful ripple effect of economic uplift, empowering yourself and others to achieve your full potential. These active steps can bring the abstract ideas of networking and collaboration into concrete action, making them understandable and useful in your journey.

4.5 Managing Finances for Startups

Alright, let's talk money, specifically how to manage it when you're just starting a business. Starting a business is exciting, but it's also incredibly challenging financially. Many promising ventures crash and burn, not because the idea was bad, but because the money ran out. It's all about understanding where your money is going, making smart choices, and planning for the unexpected. I've seen so many young entrepreneurs stumble at this hurdle, and I want to make sure you don't become one of them.

Your initial funding is your lifeline. This could come from your savings, a loan, friends, or even crowdfunding. Treat it like gold. The first thing to do is create a detailed budget, even before you officially launch. Break down every possible expense: website hosting, marketing materials, office supplies (even if it's just a corner in your room), and any software you might need. Be realistic, and always add a buffer for unforeseen costs. You'd be surprised how quickly those little expenses add up. Understand the difference between "needs" and "wants." A fancy office space might look impressive, but if it drains your cash flow, it's a want, not a need. Focus on the essentials that directly contribute to generating revenue. Use free tools and resources whenever possible; there are plenty of free software options for everything from project management to graphic design. Delay unnecessary purchases until you have a stable income stream.

Cash flow is the lifeblood of your startup. It's the money that comes in and out of your business. A positive cash flow means you have more money coming in than going out, which is essential for survival. To manage your cash flow effectively, track every single transaction, both income and expenses. There are simple accounting software options designed for beginners that can help you with this. Invoice promptly and chase up late payments. Don't be afraid to remind customers politely but firmly about outstanding invoices. Offer early payment discounts to incentivize faster payments. Negotiate payment terms with suppliers. Try to extend your payment deadlines to give yourself more breathing room. For example, instead of paying in 30 days, negotiate for 60 or even 90 days. Monitor your bank balance daily. This will give you a clear picture of your cash position and allow you to identify potential problems early on. Create a cash flow forecast. This is a projection of your expected income and expenses over a certain period. It will help you anticipate potential cash shortages and take corrective action.

Profitability is important, but it's not the only metric you should be focusing on, especially in the early stages. Many startups prioritize growth over immediate profits, focusing on building a strong customer base and market share. However, it's important to have a clear path to profitability. You must understand your unit economics, which are the revenue and costs associated with each individual sale. Calculate your customer acquisition cost (CAC). This is the cost of acquiring a new customer. Understanding your CAC will help you determine how much you can afford to spend on marketing and sales. Track your customer lifetime value (CLTV). This is the total revenue you expect to generate from a customer over the entire relationship. Comparing your CAC to your CLTV will tell you whether your business model is sustainable. Regularly review your pricing strategy. Make sure you are charging enough to cover your costs and generate a profit, but also remain competitive in the market. Identify and eliminate unnecessary expenses. Look for ways to reduce your costs without compromising the quality of your product or service.

Taxes are a reality that you must deal with from day one. Don't wait until the end of the year to think about taxes. It's important to understand your tax obligations and plan accordingly. Consult with a tax professional. A good accountant can help you navigate the complex tax laws and ensure you are taking advantage of all available deductions and credits. Keep accurate records of all income and expenses. This will make it easier to file your taxes and avoid potential penalties. Set aside money for taxes throughout the year. Don't spend all your profits; put aside a percentage to cover your estimated tax liability. Understand the different types of taxes you are responsible for, such as income tax, sales tax, and self-employment tax. Consider your business structure. The type of business structure you choose (sole proprietorship, LLC, corporation) will affect your tax obligations. Building a financial safety net for your business is crucial. Unexpected events can happen, and having a financial cushion can help you weather the storm. Establish an emergency fund. Aim to have at least three to six months' worth of operating expenses in a readily accessible account. Obtain business insurance. Protect your business from potential liabilities, such as property damage, lawsuits, and business interruption. Develop a contingency plan. This plan should outline how you will respond to various unexpected events, such as a major customer loss, a natural disaster, or an economic downturn. Diversify your revenue streams. Don't rely on a single customer or product; explore other ways to generate income. Regularly review and update your financial plans. As your business grows and evolves, your financial plans need to adapt accordingly.

5 Chapter 5: Career Pathways and Advancement

The world of work is vast and varied, more so today than ever before. It's not just about finding any job, it's about finding a path that aligns with your interests, skills, and long-term goals, particularly in light of economic circumstances that might feel limiting. Let's start with exploration. What genuinely interests you? What are you naturally good at? Don't dismiss anything offhand. Write down everything that comes to mind, even if it seems unrealistic. Think about subjects you enjoy in school, hobbies you pursue in your free time, and activities you find fulfilling. Then, consider your skills. This isn't just about formal training; it's about the things you can do well, whether it's writing, problem-solving, organizing, or communicating. Once you have a list of your interests and skills, begin researching potential career paths that combine the two. Websites like the Bureau of Labor Statistics (BLS) offer detailed information about different occupations, including job duties, education requirements, salary expectations, and job outlook. Don't limit yourself to traditional careers; explore emerging fields and industries that are growing rapidly. Consider internships, volunteering, or shadowing opportunities to gain firsthand experience in different fields and see if they are a good fit for you.

Now, let's talk about the resume, that crucial document that opens doors. It is more than just a list of your past experiences. It is a marketing tool that showcases your skills and accomplishments to potential employers. Start with a clear and concise format that is easy to read and visually appealing. Use action verbs to describe your responsibilities and achievements, and quantify your results whenever possible. For example, instead of saying "Managed social media accounts," say "Increased social media engagement by 20% in three months through targeted content creation and community management." If you lack extensive work experience, focus on highlighting your skills and accomplishments from academic projects, extracurricular activities, and volunteer work. Tailor your resume to each job you apply for, emphasizing the skills and experience that are most relevant to the specific position. Proofread carefully for any errors in grammar or spelling. Have a trusted friend, family member, or career counselor review your resume before you submit it. A well-crafted resume is your first impression, so make it count.

You've landed an interview, congratulations! Preparation is key. Research the company thoroughly. Understand their mission, values, products, and services. This will not only help you answer interview questions effectively but also demonstrate your genuine interest in the company. Practice answering common interview questions, such as "Tell me about yourself," "What are your strengths and weaknesses?" and "Why are you interested in this position?". Use the STAR method (Situation, Task, Action, Result) to structure your answers and provide specific examples of your skills and accomplishments. Prepare thoughtful questions to ask the interviewer. This shows your engagement and allows you to learn more about the role and the company culture. Choose your attire carefully. Dress professionally and appropriately for the company culture. Pay attention to your body language. Maintain eye contact, sit up straight, and smile. Be confident, enthusiastic, and genuine. Remember, an interview is a two-way street. It's an opportunity for you to assess whether the job and the company are a good fit for you, as well as for the employer to assess your qualifications.

The offer is on the table; it's time to negotiate. Salary negotiation can feel daunting, but it's a crucial step in ensuring that you are fairly compensated for your skills and experience. Before you enter negotiations, research the average salary for similar positions in your location, considering your education, experience, and skills. Websites like Glassdoor and Salary.com can provide valuable salary data. Know your worth. Determine your minimum acceptable salary and your target salary. Be prepared to justify your salary expectations based on your research and your value proposition. When the employer makes an offer, express your gratitude and enthusiasm for the opportunity. Then, politely state that you would like to discuss the salary. Don't be afraid to counteroffer. If the initial offer is lower than your target salary, provide a rationale for your counteroffer, highlighting your skills and accomplishments. Be willing to compromise. Salary is not the only factor to consider. Benefits, such as health insurance, paid time off, and retirement plans, can also significantly impact your overall compensation package. Be professional and respectful throughout the negotiation process. Remember, the goal is to reach a mutually beneficial agreement. Don't be afraid to walk away if the offer is not acceptable to you. There are other opportunities out there.

Remember, career advancement isn't a linear path. It's a journey of continuous learning, growth, and adaptation. Seek out opportunities to develop new skills and expand your knowledge. Take advantage of training programs, workshops, and online courses. Network with colleagues, mentors, and industry professionals. Attend conferences and industry events to stay up-to-date on the latest trends and developments. Be proactive in seeking out challenging assignments and responsibilities. Volunteer for projects that will stretch your skills and expose you to new areas of the business. Embrace change and be willing to adapt to new technologies and processes. Be a lifelong learner. The world of work is constantly evolving, and the more you learn, the more valuable you will become.

Finally, never underestimate the power of networking. Building relationships with people in your field is essential for career advancement. Attend industry events, join professional organizations, and connect with people online. Be proactive in reaching out to people you admire and asking for informational interviews. Don't be afraid to ask for help or advice. People are generally willing to share their knowledge and experience. Be a good listener and a valuable resource to others. Offer your assistance and support to your colleagues and mentors. Networking is a two-way street. The more you give, the more you will receive. Nurture your relationships over time. Stay in touch with people you've met, even if you don't need anything from them at the moment. You never know when a connection might lead to a new opportunity. Your network is one of your most valuable assets. Invest in it wisely. By taking these steps, you can navigate the world of work with confidence and achieve your career goals, regardless of your current circumstances.

5.1 Exploring Career Options

Choosing a career isn't just about finding a job; it's about crafting a life that resonates with your values, skills, and aspirations. For many young adults navigating current economic challenges, this decision carries even more weight. It's about finding financial stability, personal fulfillment, and a pathway to a brighter future. Let's explore the world of career possibilities, offering practical advice and inspiration to help you make informed decisions.

First, take some time for self-reflection. This involves more than just listing your skills; it's about understanding your passions, interests, and values. What truly excites you? What problems do you enjoy solving? What kind of work environment energizes you? Are you a creative thinker, a meticulous organizer, or a natural leader? Knowing your strengths and weaknesses is crucial. Don't just rely on your own perception; seek feedback from teachers, mentors, and friends. They might see qualities in you that you haven't recognized. Use online assessments like career aptitude tests, personality tests, and interest inventories to gain further insights. These tools can suggest career paths that align with your unique profile, providing a starting point for your exploration.

Beyond introspection, research is paramount. Explore various career fields and industries that pique your interest. Don't limit yourself to what's familiar; venture into unfamiliar territories. Read industry publications, browse online job boards, and watch documentaries about different professions. Talk to people working in those fields. Informational interviews are invaluable opportunities to learn firsthand about the day-to-day realities, challenges, and rewards of a particular career. Prepare thoughtful questions beforehand, focusing on their career path, the skills required, and the advice they would give to someone starting out. Shadowing professionals is another great way to gain real-world experience and observe the work environment. Consider internships, even if they are unpaid, as they provide practical skills, networking opportunities, and a clearer understanding of whether a particular career is right for you.

Consider your values and long-term goals. What kind of impact do you want to make in the world? Do you prioritize financial security, work-life balance, creative expression, or helping others? Different careers offer varying degrees of fulfillment in these areas. Think about your future aspirations. Where do you see yourself in five, ten, or twenty years? How does your chosen career align with your long-term vision? For instance, a career in social work might be deeply fulfilling if you value helping others, but it may not offer the same level of financial reward as a career in finance. Similarly, a career in the arts might provide creative freedom, but it may require a higher tolerance for uncertainty and financial instability. It's crucial to find a balance between your passions and your practical needs. Don't be afraid to explore unconventional career paths. The traditional 9-to-5 job is not the only option. Freelancing, remote work, and entrepreneurship offer greater flexibility and autonomy.

Developing skills, the need for education and training should be considered. Identify the specific skills and qualifications required for your desired career. Do you need a college degree, a

vocational certification, or on-the-job training? Research the educational pathways available and the associated costs. Consider alternative learning options, such as online courses, community college programs, and apprenticeships, which can be more affordable and accessible than traditional four-year colleges. Look for opportunities to develop your skills through volunteer work, extracurricular activities, and personal projects. A strong portfolio of work can be just as valuable as a formal education in certain fields. Network with professionals in your desired field. Attend industry events, join professional organizations, and connect with people on social media. Building relationships can open doors to internships, mentorships, and job opportunities.
Consider the job market. Research the current and projected demand for different occupations in your region and beyond. Look for industries that are experiencing growth and innovation. Consider the impact of technology on the future of work. Which skills are becoming more valuable in the digital age? Which jobs are at risk of automation? Adaptability and lifelong learning are essential for navigating the ever-changing job market. Be prepared to update your skills and knowledge throughout your career. Embrace new technologies and be open to exploring new career paths as they emerge. Think about the location of job opportunities. Are you willing to relocate for a better career prospect? Some industries are concentrated in certain geographic areas. Consider the cost of living and quality of life in different loca-

tions. A lower salary in a more affordable city might be more appealing than a higher salary in an expensive urban area.

Career planning is an ongoing process, not a one-time event. Be prepared to reassess your goals and make adjustments along the way. It's okay to change your mind or pursue a different path. Many successful people have had multiple careers throughout their lives. Don't be afraid to take risks and try new things. The most important thing is to stay curious, keep learning, and never stop exploring your potential. Finding the right career takes time, effort, and persistence. Don't get discouraged by setbacks or rejections. View them as learning opportunities and keep moving forward. Surround yourself with a supportive network of friends, family, and mentors who can offer encouragement and guidance. Remember that your career is just one aspect of your life. It's important to maintain a healthy work-life balance and prioritize your well-being. Find activities that bring you joy and fulfillment outside of work. A fulfilling career is one that aligns with your values, passions, and goals, while also providing financial security and personal growth.

Remember, your journey to finding the right career is unique to you. There's no one-size-fits-all solution. Be patient, stay persistent, and trust your instincts. With careful planning, self-awareness, and a willingness to learn, you can create a fulfilling and successful career that empowers you to thrive.

5.2 Resume Building & Interview Skills

Crafting a compelling resume and mastering interview skills are crucial stepping stones on your path to economic upliftment. They are the tools that unlock doors and showcase your potential to the world. Let's delve into how you can effectively present yourself to potential employers and land that dream job.

Your resume is your personal marketing document, a concise summary of your skills, experience, and education. It's often the first impression you make, so make it count. Start with a clean and professional template; avoid overly fancy designs that can distract from the content. At the top, include your full name, phone number, email address, and a professional-looking LinkedIn profile URL if you have one. Next, craft a compelling summary or objective statement. A summary highlights your key skills and experience, while an objective focuses on your career goals. As a young adult, an objective might be more appropriate if you're just starting out, clearly stating the type of role you're seeking. Think of it as a very short elevator pitch. Then, comes your experience section. Even if you haven't held traditional jobs, include volunteer work, internships, and even relevant school projects. Use action verbs to describe your accomplishments, and quantify your achievements whenever possible. Instead of saying "Helped with fundraising," say "Raised $500 for [Organization Name] through online campaigns." Be specific and results-oriented. Next up, your education section is essential. List your high school, any vocational training, or college (if applicable), your GPA if it's above a 3.0, and any relevant coursework or honors you received. Remember to list any skills that you might have. Tailor your resume to each job application, highlighting the skills and experiences that are most relevant to the specific position. Use keywords from the job description to ensure your resume gets noticed by applicant tracking systems. Now that you have a polished resume, it's time to prepare for the interview. Remember, the interview is your chance to bring your resume to life and demonstrate your personality, enthusiasm, and fit for the company culture. Before the interview, research the company thoroughly. Understand their mission, values, products/services, and recent news. This will enable you to speak intelligently about the organization and demonstrate your genuine interest. Prepare answers to common interview questions. These include "Tell me about yourself," "What are your strengths and weaknesses?" "Why are you interested in this position?" and "Where do you see yourself in five years?" Practice your answers out loud, but don't memorize them word-for-word. You want to sound natural and conversational.

During the interview, make a strong first impression. Dress professionally, arrive on time (or even a few minutes early), and greet the interviewer with a warm smile and a firm handshake. Maintain eye contact and listen attentively to the interviewer's questions. When answering questions, use the STAR method: Situation, Task, Action, Result. Describe the situation you were in, the task you were assigned, the actions you took, and the results you achieved. This framework helps you provide clear and concise answers that demonstrate your skills and accomplishments. Be enthusiastic and show your passion for the opportunity. Let your personality shine through, and be yourself. Ask thoughtful questions. Asking questions demonstrates your engagement and genuine interest in the company and the role. Prepare a few questions in advance, such as "What are the biggest challenges facing the team right now?" or "What opportunities are there for professional development?" After the interview, send a thank-you note to the interviewer within 24 hours. Express your gratitude for their time and reiterate your interest in the position. You can also use this opportunity to clarify any points from the interview or provide additional information.

Beyond the basics, consider the power of networking. Even before you actively seek out jobs, building connections is a game-changer. Attend career fairs, workshops, and industry events to meet professionals in your field of interest. Join relevant student organizations or professional associations. Networking isn't just about asking for jobs; it's about building relationships. Connect with people on LinkedIn, engage in meaningful conversations, and offer your support to others. Don't be afraid to reach out to people for informational interviews. An informational interview is a casual conversation where you can learn about someone's career path, gain insights into a particular industry, and ask for advice.

Your online presence matters. Employers often check candidates' social media profiles, so ensure yours presents a positive and professional image. Remove any inappropriate content, and showcase your skills and interests through your LinkedIn profile and other online platforms. Consider creating a personal website or online portfolio to showcase your work and accomplishments. This is a great way to stand out from the competition and demonstrate your initiative.

Furthermore, never underestimate the power of practice. Participate in mock interviews with friends, family, or career counselors. This will help you become more comfortable with the interview process and identify areas for improvement. Record yourself answering common interview questions and review the footage to identify any nervous habits or areas where you can improve your communication skills. Seek feedback from mentors and trusted advisors. They can provide valuable insights and help you refine your resume and interview skills. Don't be discouraged by rejections. Job searching can be a challenging process, and rejection is a normal part of it. Learn from your mistakes, refine your approach, and keep moving forward. Remember, every "no" brings you closer to a "yes." Finally, build your confidence. Believe in yourself and your abilities. You have unique skills and experiences to offer, and you deserve to find a job that fulfills you and helps you achieve your goals. Visualize success, practice positive self-talk, and surround yourself with supportive people who believe in you.

Crafting your resume and mastering interview skills isn't just about landing a job; it's about investing in your future. By presenting yourself effectively, building a strong network, and believing in your potential, you'll be well-equipped to navigate the job market and achieve your career aspirations. This proactive approach is a powerful step toward achieving lasting economic upliftment. Now go out there and show the world what you're capable of.

5.3 Negotiating Salaries

Negotiating salaries can feel daunting, especially when you're just starting your career. Many young people undersell themselves, leaving money on the table simply because they don't know how to effectively advocate for their worth. This chapter isn't about becoming a ruthless negotiator; it's about understanding your value and confidently communicating it to your employer. It's a skill that will benefit you throughout your career, leading to greater financial security and a feeling of being valued for your contributions.

Before you even reach the negotiation stage, thorough preparation is paramount. Research is your best friend. Begin by understanding the average salary range for your role and experience level in your specific geographic location. Websites like Glassdoor, Salary.com, and Payscale can provide valuable insights. Don't rely solely on one source; cross-reference the information to get a more accurate picture. Beyond salary, consider the entire compensation package. This includes benefits such as health insurance, retirement plans, paid time off, stock options, and professional development opportunities. Assign a monetary value to each benefit to get a true understanding of your potential earnings. For instance, a comprehensive health insurance plan can save you thousands of dollars annually.

Once you have a clear understanding of the market rate, honestly assess your skills and experience. What unique qualities do you bring to the table? Have you exceeded expectations in previous roles or projects? Quantify your accomplishments whenever possible. For example, instead of saying "I improved customer satisfaction," say "I improved customer satisfaction scores by 15% within six months." Numbers speak volumes and demonstrate the tangible impact you've made. Think about the specific needs of the company and how your skills directly address those needs. This will allow you to tailor your negotiation points and highlight your value proposition. Consider what you're truly willing to accept as your minimum salary. Having this number in mind will prevent you from being pressured into accepting an offer that doesn't meet your financial needs.

The actual negotiation is a conversation, not a confrontation. When the offer comes, express your gratitude and enthusiasm for the opportunity. This sets a positive tone and demonstrates your genuine interest in the role. Take your time to review the offer carefully and don't feel pressured to accept it immediately. A polite, "Thank you for the offer. I'd like some time to review it carefully," is perfectly acceptable. When you're ready to respond, start by reiterating your enthusiasm for the role and the company. Then, smoothly transition into your counter-offer. Frame your request as an investment in the company's success. Explain how your skills and experience will contribute to the organization's goals and justify your desired salary. Be prepared to provide data and examples to support your request.

Be confident, but also be flexible. Negotiation is about finding a mutually beneficial agreement. You may not get everything you want, but you should aim for a compensation package that fairly reflects your value. If the company is unable to meet your salary expectations, explore other options. Perhaps they can offer a signing bonus, performance-based bonuses, additional vacation time, or opportunities for professional development. These perks can significantly increase the overall value of the compensation package. During the negotiation, listen actively to the employer's concerns and be willing to compromise. Show them that you're a team player and that you're committed to finding a solution that works for everyone. If you reach an impasse, don't be afraid to walk away. Knowing your worth and being prepared to decline an offer that doesn't meet your needs demonstrates confidence and professionalism.

Finally, practice makes perfect. Rehearse your negotiation points with a friend or mentor. This will help you feel more confident and articulate during the actual conversation. Anticipate potential objections and prepare your responses in advance. Remember to remain calm and professional, even if the negotiation becomes challenging. Your attitude and demeanor can significantly impact the outcome. Even after you've accepted an offer, continue to network and develop your skills. The job market is constantly evolving, so it's important to stay informed and adapt to new trends. Continuously improving your skills and knowledge will make you a more valuable asset to any organization, increasing your earning potential in the long run. Salary negotiation is a skill that requires practice and patience, but it's an investment that will pay off throughout your career. Don't be afraid to advocate for your worth and strive for a compensation package that reflects your true value.

6 Chapter 6: Building a Strong Support System

Economic empowerment is rarely a solo act. It's a symphony of connections, guidance, and shared experiences. Building a strong support system is paramount. It's the safety net that catches you when you stumble, the sounding board that amplifies your ideas, and the compass that helps you navigate uncharted waters. For young adults striving to transcend economic limitations, this network isn't a luxury; it's a necessity. It allows you to leverage the experiences and wisdom of others, expanding your horizons beyond your immediate circumstances.

Mentorship and guidance serve as the bedrock of a solid support structure. Think of a mentor as a seasoned traveler who's already navigated the terrain you're about to explore. Their experiences, both triumphs and setbacks, can provide invaluable insights, saving you time and energy. Seek mentors who align with your aspirations. This could be a successful entrepreneur in your community, a professor who inspires you, or even a family member who has overcome similar challenges. The key is to find someone who is willing to invest their time and knowledge in your growth. This journey starts with identifying potential mentors. Reflect on the individuals who have positively influenced you – those whose accomplishments you admire, and whose values resonate with your own. Don't be afraid to reach out! A simple email or a brief conversation expressing your admiration and asking for advice can be the first step. Be prepared to articulate your goals and demonstrate a genuine desire to learn. A mentor is more likely to invest in someone who is proactive and committed to their own development. Remember, the mentorship dynamic is a two-way street. While you'll be receiving guidance, you also have the opportunity to offer fresh perspectives and contribute to the relationship. Regular communication is vital. Schedule consistent check-ins, whether it's a monthly coffee meeting or a weekly phone call. Use this time to discuss your progress, challenges, and seek advice on specific issues. Be open to feedback, even if it's difficult to hear. Constructive criticism is essential for growth.

Networking, often perceived as a daunting task, is simply the art of building relationships. It's about connecting with people who share your interests, values, or career aspirations. Don't think of networking as a transactional exchange of business cards. Instead, focus on building genuine connections based on mutual respect and shared goals. Think of it as cultivating a garden.

You plant seeds (initial connections), nurture them (regular communication), and watch them grow into valuable relationships. Start small. Attend local community events, workshops, or seminars related to your field of interest. These gatherings provide opportunities to meet like-minded individuals in a relaxed and informal setting. Prepare an "elevator pitch" – a concise and compelling summary of your skills and aspirations. This allows you to quickly introduce yourself and make a memorable impression. Listen more than you talk. Ask questions, show genuine interest in others, and remember their names. People are more likely to connect with someone who is genuinely interested in them. Embrace online platforms. LinkedIn, for example, is a powerful tool for building professional connections. Join relevant groups, participate in discussions, and connect with individuals in your field. Remember to personalize your connection requests. A generic message is less likely to be accepted. Follow up after meeting someone new. Send a thank-you email or a LinkedIn connection request, referencing something you discussed during your conversation. This shows that you value the connection and are interested in building a relationship. Networking isn't a one-time event. It's an ongoing process of building and nurturing relationships over time. Stay in touch with your network, even if you don't need anything from them at the moment. Offer your help, share relevant information, and celebrate their successes. A strong network is built on mutual support and reciprocity.

Leveraging online communities is also beneficial. The internet offers a wealth of resources and support networks for young adults navigating economic challenges. Online forums, social media groups, and virtual mentorship programs can connect you with peers who understand your struggles and can offer valuable advice and encouragement. Seek out communities that align with your interests and goals. These could be groups focused on entrepreneurship, personal finance, or specific career paths. Participate actively in discussions, share your experiences, and offer your support to others. Don't be afraid to ask for help. Many online communities have experienced professionals who are willing to offer guidance and mentorship. Be mindful of the information you share online. Protect your privacy and avoid posting anything that could damage your reputation.

Remember, building a strong support system is an investment in your future. It requires effort, patience, and a willingness to connect with others. But the rewards are immeasurable. A strong support system can provide you with the confidence, resources, and guidance you need to overcome economic limitations and achieve your full potential. Economic uplift is not a solitary endeavor, it's a collaborative process of shared knowledge, experience, and mutual support. Embrace the power of connection, and build a network that empowers you to thrive.

It's also important to be proactive in seeking out resources. Don't wait for opportunities to come to you; actively seek them out. Research local community organizations that offer financial assistance, career counseling, or mentorship programs. Attend workshops and seminars that can enhance your skills and knowledge. Network with professionals in your field to learn about job opportunities and industry trends. The more proactive you are, the more likely you are to find the resources and support you need to succeed. Remember that persistence is key. You may encounter setbacks and challenges along the way, but don't give up on your goals. Stay focused, remain resilient, and continue to seek out opportunities for growth and development. With a strong support system and a proactive mindset, you can overcome economic limitations and create a brighter future for yourself.

Ultimately, you're not just building a network; you're building a foundation. A foundation of resilience, knowledge, and shared experience. This foundation will not only support you in times of difficulty but will also propel you forward as you pursue your dreams and aspirations. So, embrace the power of connection, cultivate your relationships, and build a support system that empowers you to thrive. Remember that success isn't just about what you achieve, it's about who you become along the way, and the people who helped you get there. By prioritizing your support system, you're not only investing in your financial future, you're investing in your personal growth and overall well-being.

6.1 Mentorship and Guidance

Finding someone who's been where you're trying to go can feel like striking gold. Mentorship isn't just about having someone older or more experienced tell you what to do; it's about building a relationship with someone who can offer guidance, support, and honest feedback as you navigate your economic journey. It's about having someone in your corner, cheering you on while also holding you accountable. In many ways, it can be like having a personal GPS for your financial life, someone who can help you course-correct when you inevitably veer off track.

So, how do you actually find this "gold," this mentor who can help you unlock your economic potential? It starts with identifying what you need. Are you struggling with budgeting? Do you want to start a business but don't know where to begin? Are you trying to figure out how to invest wisely? Knowing your specific needs will help you target individuals who possess the expertise and experience to guide you in those areas. Think about people you admire, those who have achieved success in fields that interest you. This could be teachers, community leaders, local business owners, or even alumni from your school. Don't be afraid to reach out! Many people are happy to share their knowledge and experience with young people who are eager to learn. The worst they can say is no, and you'll be no worse off than you were before. Consider platforms your school provides, or community organizations that offer mentorship programs. Structured programs can offer a safe and supportive environment, pairing you with a mentor who has been carefully vetted. However, don't limit yourself to formal programs. Sometimes the best mentors are those you find organically through your own networking efforts.

Now, let's talk about making the most of a mentoring relationship. Once you've found a mentor, it's important to establish clear expectations. Discuss your goals, how often you'd like to meet, and what you hope to gain from the relationship. Come prepared to each meeting with specific questions and topics to discuss. Remember, your mentor is giving you their time and expertise, so make it count. I suggest that you be proactive and engaged. Don't expect your mentor to spoon-feed you all the answers. Take initiative, do your research, and come ready to discuss your ideas and challenges. A good mentor will guide you, but they won't do the work for you. Also, actively listen to your mentor's advice, and be open to feedback, even if it's difficult to hear. Mentors have a wealth of experience, and their insights can be invaluable. However, don't feel obligated to follow their advice blindly. Ultimately, you are responsible for your own decisions, and you should always weigh your mentor's advice against your own judgment and values.

Furthermore, remember that mentorship is a two-way street. While you are primarily benefiting from your mentor's guidance, look for ways to give back. Offer to help them with small tasks, share your own knowledge and experiences, or simply express your gratitude for their time and support. Building a strong relationship with your mentor can open doors to opportunities you never thought possible. Your mentor can introduce you to their network, provide you with valuable insights into your chosen field, and even advocate for you when opportunities arise. Treat your mentor with respect, and cherish the relationship you have built. It is a relationship that is mutually beneficial, and can last for decades to come.

In addition to formal mentorship relationships, there are other avenues for seeking guidance and support. Look for role models who inspire you, even if you don't have a direct connection with them. Read their books, watch their interviews, and learn from their experiences. Attend workshops, seminars, and conferences in your field of interest. These events can provide you with valuable knowledge, skills, and networking opportunities. You can also tap into the power of online communities and forums. There are countless online groups dedicated to various topics, from personal finance to entrepreneurship. These communities can provide you with a supportive network of peers who are facing similar challenges and can offer valuable advice and encouragement. If you use social media, following leaders and influencers in your field is a great way to broaden your understanding of subjects that matter to you.

Cultivating a supportive network is crucial for overcoming economic limitations. Remember, you are not alone on this journey. There are people who care about your success and are willing to help you achieve your goals. Don't be afraid to reach out, ask for help, and build relationships with those who can support you along the way. Your mentor can assist with all of this, if you find the right one.

Finally, I want to share a personal story. When I was starting out, I had no idea how to navigate the world of business. I was lucky enough to connect with a local entrepreneur who took me under his wing. He taught me the importance of hard work, perseverance, and never giving up on my dreams. He also introduced me to his network of contacts, which opened doors to opportunities that I never thought possible. Without his guidance and support, I wouldn't be where I am today. His mentorship was one of the most important things in my life.

So, take the initiative to find a mentor, build a strong support system, and never stop learning and growing. With the right guidance and support, you can overcome any economic limitations and achieve your full potential. I know it can be challenging, but I have faith in you. You have the power to transform your life and create a brighter future for yourself.

6.2 Networking Effectively

Networking isn't just about collecting business cards; it's about cultivating genuine relationships that can open doors you never knew existed. As someone who once felt completely out of my depth at a professional event, trust me, I understand how intimidating it can be. But I've learned that with a little preparation and the right mindset, anyone can become a proficient networker. The key is to approach it as an opportunity to learn and connect with others, not just as a means to an end.

Before even stepping foot into a networking event or sending that first introductory email, take some time to identify your goals. What are you hoping to achieve through networking? Are you looking for a mentor, seeking internship opportunities, or trying to learn more about a specific industry? Having a clear purpose will help you focus your efforts and make your interactions more meaningful. Research the event or the people you plan to connect with beforehand. Knowing their background, interests, or recent accomplishments can provide valuable talking points and demonstrate your genuine interest. For example, if you're attending a conference on sustainable energy, research the speakers and exhibitors beforehand. Identify individuals whose work resonates with you and prepare thoughtful questions to ask them. This shows that you've done your homework and are genuinely interested in learning from them.

Now, let's talk about making a strong first impression. Body language speaks volumes. Maintain eye contact, offer a firm handshake (when appropriate), and smile genuinely. Project confidence, even if you're feeling nervous. Introduce yourself clearly and state your name and affiliation. Avoid rambling or speaking too quickly. Listen attentively when others are speaking and show genuine interest in what they have to say. Ask open-ended questions to encourage them to elaborate and share their experiences. Remember, networking is a two-way street. It's about building a reciprocal relationship, not just about promoting yourself. When someone shares their experiences or insights, offer your own relevant perspectives or experiences in return. This demonstrates that you're actively engaged in the conversation and have something valuable to contribute. It will create a better impression than simply waiting for your turn to speak.

Beyond events, leverage the power of online platforms like LinkedIn to expand your network and connect with professionals in your field. Craft a professional profile that highlights your skills, experiences, and career aspirations. Actively participate in relevant groups and discussions, sharing your insights and engaging with others. Don't be afraid to reach out to people directly, but always personalize your messages. Avoid generic connection requests. Instead, explain why you're interested in connecting and what you hope to gain from the relationship. For instance, you could say, "I've been following your work in renewable energy for some time, and I'm particularly impressed with your work on solar panel efficiency. I'm a student interested in pursuing a career in this field, and I would be grateful for the opportunity to learn more about your experiences." I have seen this work better than the generic requests.

Follow-up is crucial. After meeting someone at an event or connecting with them online, send a personalized thank-you note or email within 24-48 hours. Reinforce the key takeaways from your conversation and express your interest in staying connected. Offer to provide value to them in some way, such as sharing a relevant article or connecting them with someone in your network.

Remember, networking is not a one-time event. It's an ongoing process of building and nurturing relationships. Stay in touch with your contacts regularly, even if you don't have a specific agenda. Share interesting articles, congratulate them on their accomplishments, or simply check in to see how they're doing. By staying top-of-mind, you'll strengthen your relationships and create opportunities for future collaboration.

It's important to understand that networking is not about immediate gratification. It's about building long-term relationships that can benefit you both personally and professionally. Don't expect to get a job offer or a business deal after every networking event. Instead, focus on building genuine connections and fostering a spirit of collaboration. Be patient, persistent, and authentic. Eventually, your efforts will pay off in unexpected ways. Remember that rejections are a normal part of the process. Not everyone you reach out to will respond, and not every connection will lead to a meaningful relationship. Don't take it personally. Learn from your experiences and keep moving forward. The more you network, the more comfortable and confident you'll become. It's like any other skill – the more you practice, the better you'll get. Also, remember that networking is not just about what you can get from others, it's about what you can give. Be generous with your time, knowledge, and resources. Offer to help others in your network whenever possible. By giving back, you'll build goodwill and strengthen your relationships.

Be aware of cultural differences and communication styles. What is considered appropriate in one culture may be inappropriate in another. Take the time to learn about the customs and etiquette of different cultures before networking with people from diverse backgrounds. Networking is an ongoing process, not a one-time event. Stay in touch with your contacts regularly, even if you don't have a specific agenda. Share interesting articles, congratulate them on their accomplishments, or simply check in to see how they're doing. If possible, find ways to meet your contacts in person. A face-to-face meeting can help strengthen your connection and build trust.

Ultimately, successful networking is about building genuine relationships based on mutual respect and trust. It's about connecting with people on a human level, sharing your passions and interests, and supporting each other's goals. When you approach networking with authenticity and a genuine desire to connect with others, you'll be surprised at the doors that open and the opportunities that arise. I am sure you will master this art if you are consistent.

7 Chapter 7: Long-Term Financial Planning

Looking ahead, far beyond graduation and your first job, is crucial. It may seem distant and even a little intimidating, but understanding the basics of long-term financial planning now can set you up for a more secure and comfortable future. We're not talking about becoming a Wall Street wizard overnight, but rather building a foundation of knowledge that allows you to make informed decisions about your money. This isn't about getting rich quick, but about building wealth slowly and steadily, over time. Investing, at its core, is simply putting your money to work for you. Instead of letting it sit in a savings account earning minimal interest, you use it to purchase assets that have the potential to grow in value over time. The stock market, often portrayed in movies and television as a chaotic and risky place, can be a powerful tool for long-term growth if approached with knowledge and caution. Stocks represent ownership in a company, and their value can increase as the company grows and becomes more profitable. Bonds, on the other hand, are essentially loans you make to a government or corporation. They typically offer lower returns than stocks but are considered less risky. Mutual funds and Exchange-Traded Funds (ETFs) are baskets of stocks and bonds, offering instant diversification and reducing your overall risk. Spreading your investments across different asset classes is a key principle of long-term investing, minimizing the impact of any single investment performing poorly. Before diving in, take some time to research different investment options and understand their associated risks and potential rewards. Online resources, financial websites, and even introductory books can be invaluable in this process. Start small, perhaps with a small amount of money you're comfortable losing, and gradually increase your investments as you gain more experience and confidence. Remember, the key to successful investing is patience and a long-term perspective. Don't be swayed by short-term market fluctuations or get-rich-quick schemes. Stick to your investment plan, rebalance your portfolio periodically, and let compounding do its magic over time.

Beyond investing, one of the most important aspects of long-term financial planning is retirement planning. It might seem a million miles away when you are busy thinking about the next exam, but establishing an early idea of potential needs for when you stop working can be extremely valuable. Retirement accounts, such as 401(k)s and IRAs (Individual Retirement Accounts), offer tax advantages that can help you grow your savings faster. A 401(k) is typically offered through your employer, and many employers will match a portion of your contributions, essentially giving you free money. An IRA is an individual account that you can open yourself, offering more flexibility in terms of investment options. The power of compounding is especially potent when it comes to retirement savings. Starting early, even with small contributions, can make a huge difference in the long run. For example, contributing just a few hundred dollars per month starting in your twenties can potentially result in hundreds of thousands of dollars saved by the time you retire. Consider your lifestyle, expenses, and desired retirement age when determining how much you need to save. Use online retirement calculators to estimate your future needs and adjust your savings plan accordingly. Remember, it's always better to overestimate than underestimate when it comes to retirement savings.

While it might seem morbid to consider, estate planning is an essential part of long-term financial security, and it is important to have it in order. It involves making arrangements for the distribution of your assets after your death and ensuring that your wishes are carried out. A will is a legal document that outlines how you want your property to be distributed, who will be the guardian of your minor children (if applicable), and who will be responsible for managing your estate. Without a will, the state will determine how your assets are distributed, which may not align with your wishes. A power of attorney is a legal document that grants someone else the authority to make financial or medical decisions on your behalf if you become incapacitated. This can be especially important if you become unable to manage your own affairs due to illness or injury. A living will, also known as an advance healthcare directive, outlines your wishes regarding medical treatment in the event that you are unable to communicate your decisions. This can help ensure that you receive the type of care you want and avoid unwanted medical interventions. While you may not have significant assets at this stage in your life, it's still important to have these basic estate planning documents in place. As your assets grow and your circumstances change, you can update these documents to reflect your current situation. Consulting with an attorney specializing in estate planning can provide valuable guidance and ensure that your wishes are legally protected.

Furthermore, consider insurance as an integral part of your long-term financial plan. Health insurance protects you from the potentially devastating costs of medical care. Life insurance provides financial support to your loved ones in the event of your death. Disability insurance replaces a portion of your income if you become unable to work due to illness or injury. These are all vital components of a solid long term financial plan.

Financial planning is not a one-size-fits-all solution. Everyone's circumstances, goals, and risk tolerance are different. What works for one person may not work for another. Therefore, it's important to tailor your financial plan to your specific needs and aspirations. This might involve seeking advice from a qualified financial advisor who can help you assess your situation, identify your goals, and develop a customized plan that aligns with your unique circumstances.

Ultimately, long-term financial planning is about taking control of your financial future and building a secure and prosperous life. It's about making informed decisions, saving diligently, and investing wisely. It's about protecting yourself from financial risks and ensuring that your loved ones are taken care of. It's about creating a future where you can pursue your dreams without financial worries. By starting early and embracing the principles of long-term financial planning, you can set yourself on a path towards financial freedom and achieve your lifelong goals.

7.1 Investing for the Future

Let's talk about making your money work for you in the long run. Thinking about the future might seem distant when you're juggling school, work, and everything else, but starting to invest now, even with small amounts, can make a huge difference down the road. Time is one of the most powerful tools you have on your side. Investing early allows your money to grow through the power of compounding. This means that you earn returns not only on your initial investment but also on the accumulated interest or gains over time.

Investing is essentially buying a small piece of a company or asset with the expectation that its value will increase over time. It's about putting your money to work instead of letting it sit idle in a savings account, where inflation can erode its purchasing power. There are many different types of investments, but a few of the most common include stocks, bonds, and mutual funds. Stocks represent ownership in a company, and their value can fluctuate based on the company's performance and market conditions. Bonds are essentially loans you make to a company or government, and they typically offer a fixed rate of return. Mutual funds pool money from multiple investors to invest in a diversified portfolio of stocks, bonds, or other assets, offering instant diversification and professional management.

Now, you might be thinking, "I don't have a lot of money to invest." That's perfectly okay! You don't need to be rich to start investing. The key is to start small and be consistent. Many brokerage firms offer accounts with no minimum balance requirements, and some even allow you to buy fractional shares of stocks, meaning you can invest in companies like Apple or Google with just a few dollars. Dollar-cost averaging is a great strategy for beginners. It involves investing a fixed amount of money at regular intervals, regardless of the market's performance. This helps to smooth out the ups and downs of the market and reduces the risk of buying high and selling low. For instance, you might invest $50 every month into a specific mutual fund.

Before you start investing, it's important to understand your risk tolerance. Risk tolerance refers to your comfort level with the possibility of losing money in exchange for the potential of higher returns. Generally, younger investors with a longer time horizon can afford to take on more risk, while older investors closer to retirement may prefer a more conservative approach. Consider your financial goals, time horizon, and personal preferences when determining your risk tolerance. A risk assessment questionnaire can be a useful tool to gauge your risk appetite. When determining your risk tolerance, take into account that some investment plans can be quite risky. The goal of investing should be to increase your personal wealth while minimizing your risk.

Once you understand your risk tolerance, you can choose investments that align with your comfort level. Diversification is a key strategy for managing risk. It involves spreading your investments across different asset classes, industries, and geographic regions. This helps to reduce the impact of any single investment on your overall portfolio. For example, instead of putting all your money into one stock, you could invest in a mix of stocks, bonds, and real estate. Exchange-Traded Funds (ETFs) are another excellent way to diversify your portfolio. ETFs are similar to mutual funds, but they trade on stock exchanges like individual stocks, offering greater flexibility and often lower expense ratios.

It's crucial to do your research before investing in any company or asset. Understand the business model, financial performance, and industry trends. Read company reports, listen to investor calls, and consult with financial advisors if needed. Don't invest in something you don't understand. There are numerous online resources available to help you research investments, including financial news websites, brokerage firm research reports, and independent investment analysis platforms. Consider the investment's expense ratio or management fees. These fees can eat into your returns over time, so it's important to choose low-cost options whenever possible. Index funds, which track a specific market index like the S&P 500, typically have lower expense ratios than actively managed funds.

It's important to remember that investing is a long-term game. There will be ups and downs in the market, but it's crucial to stay focused on your long-term goals and avoid making impulsive decisions based on short-term market fluctuations. Don't panic sell when the market dips. Instead, view market downturns as opportunities to buy quality investments at discounted prices. Rebalancing your portfolio periodically is also important. Rebalancing involves adjusting your asset allocation to maintain your desired risk level. For example, if your stock allocation has grown too large due to market gains, you might sell some stocks and buy more bonds to bring your portfolio back into balance. Stay informed about market trends and economic developments, but don't let the daily news overwhelm you. Focus on the fundamentals of investing and stick to your long-term plan. Continuously educate yourself about investing. Read books, articles, and blogs, attend seminars, and consider taking online courses to improve your financial literacy. The more you know, the better equipped you'll be to make informed investment decisions. Also, don't be afraid to seek professional advice. A financial advisor can help you develop a personalized investment plan based on your individual circumstances and goals. Remember, investing is a journey, not a destination. The most important thing is to start early, stay consistent, and be patient. The rewards of long-term investing can be significant.

7.2 Retirement Planning Basics

The journey to a comfortable retirement might seem impossibly distant when you're a young adult, especially when navigating the immediate pressures of education, career, and daily expenses. But time is your greatest ally, and understanding the fundamental principles of retirement planning now can make a monumental difference in your future financial security. Forget the complex jargon for now. We're talking about laying a simple, solid foundation.

Start by visualizing your ideal retirement. What does it look like?

Where do you live? What activities fill your days? Do you envision traveling the world, pursuing hobbies, or simply relaxing and spending time with loved ones? This isn't just daydreaming; it's about setting a tangible goal. Quantify that vision as best you can, even crudely. Imagine what your living expenses will be – accounting for inflation is crucial. There are numerous online inflation calculators to help estimate this. Start with current costs of things like rent, groceries, healthcare, and entertainment, and project how those costs might increase over several decades. This rough estimate, even if inaccurate, is a starting point for determining how much you'll need to save. Consider consulting online resources to get a general range or to speak with a financial advisor.

Next, consider the various retirement accounts available to you. The options can feel overwhelming, but don't be discouraged. The two main categories are employer-sponsored plans like 401(k)s and individual retirement accounts (IRAs). If your employer offers a 401(k), especially with a matching contribution, that's almost always the first place to start. That matching contribution is essentially free money, and passing it up is like turning down a raise. Participate at least enough to get the full match, even if it means making small sacrifices elsewhere. If your employer doesn't offer a 401(k), or you want to save more, an IRA is an excellent option. There are two primary types: traditional and Roth. With a traditional IRA, contributions may be tax-deductible, and your earnings grow tax-deferred, meaning you don't pay taxes until you withdraw the money in retirement. With a Roth IRA, contributions are made with after-tax dollars, but your earnings and withdrawals in retirement are tax-free. Which one is better? It depends on your individual circumstances and expectations for future tax rates. If you anticipate being in a higher tax bracket in retirement, a Roth IRA might be more advantageous.

Investment choices within these accounts can be equally daunting, but the key is diversification. Don't put all your eggs in one basket. A simple, low-cost strategy for beginners is to invest in a diversified portfolio of index funds or exchange-traded funds (ETFs) that track broad market indexes like the S&P 500 or the total stock market. These funds offer instant diversification across hundreds or thousands of companies, reducing your risk. Over time, you can adjust your asset allocation (the mix of stocks, bonds, and other assets) as you get closer to retirement. When you are young, you can take slightly more risk, and as you get older you should take less.

Let's talk about the magic of compound interest. It's a concept Albert Einstein supposedly called the "eighth wonder of the world." It's essentially earning interest on your interest, and it's what allows your money to grow exponentially over time. The earlier you start saving, the more time your money has to compound. Even small contributions made consistently over many years can

accumulate into a substantial nest egg. For instance, if you start saving just $100 per month at age 22, and your investments earn an average annual return of 7%, you could potentially have over $300,000 by age 67. Increase that to $200, and that number rises even more. It's not about getting rich quickly; it's about building wealth slowly and steadily over the long haul. Don't focus on how much you're earning, focus on how long it is taking.
Finally, make retirement planning a regular part of your financial life. Review your progress annually, adjust your contributions as needed, and stay informed about changes in tax laws and investment options. Don't be afraid to seek professional advice from a qualified financial advisor, but remember that you are ultimately responsible for your own financial future. Retirement planning is a marathon, not a sprint. Starting early, staying consistent, and making informed decisions along the way will significantly increase your chances of achieving your retirement goals.

7.3 Estate Planning Overview

Think about securing everything you've worked hard for; it's more than just money—it's your legacy, your peace of mind, and how you care for those you love even when you're not around. Estate planning might sound intimidating, but at its core, it's about taking control and making informed decisions. For young adults, it may seem distant, yet it's an important part of securing your future.

One of the first elements to consider when thinking about your estate is a will. This document dictates who receives your assets – from savings accounts to personal possessions – after you're gone. Without a will, state laws determine how your assets are distributed, which might not align with your wishes. For instance, if you have specific sentimental items you want to leave to particular friends or family members, a will is essential. If you're wondering where to start, many online resources can guide you through the process, or you can consult with an estate planning attorney. The key thing is to make sure your will is legally sound and reflects your current circumstances. If you're just starting out, this might seem unnecessary, but it offers peace of mind knowing that your wishes will be respected. Remember, you can always update your will as your life evolves, adding new beneficiaries or revising asset distributions as needed.

Beyond a will, consider setting up a power of attorney. This legal document allows you to designate someone to make financial or medical decisions on your behalf if you become incapacitated. There are different types of powers of attorney, including durable power of attorney, which remains in effect even if you become mentally incapacitated. Imagine a scenario where you're traveling abroad and become seriously ill; a power of attorney would allow your designated agent to access your bank accounts to pay for medical expenses or manage your affairs back home. Deciding who to appoint as your power of attorney is a significant decision. Choose someone you trust implicitly, someone who understands your values and will act in your best interest. Discuss your wishes with them beforehand, so they are well-prepared to make decisions that align with your preferences.

Another aspect of estate planning is beneficiary designations. Many financial accounts, such as retirement accounts, life insurance policies, and investment accounts, allow you to name beneficiaries who will receive the assets directly upon your death. These designations override your will, so it's essential to keep them up to date. For example, if you get married or divorced, or if you have children, you'll want to review and update your beneficiary designations accordingly. Take the time to log into your financial accounts and verify that your beneficiaries are accurately listed. It's also wise to name contingent beneficiaries, who will receive the assets if your primary beneficiary is unable to.

For more complex situations, consider establishing a trust. A trust is a legal arrangement where you transfer assets to a trustee, who manages them for the benefit of your beneficiaries. Trusts can offer several advantages, including avoiding probate, which is the legal process of validating a will. They can also provide asset protection and tax benefits. There are different types of trusts, such as revocable trusts, which you can modify or revoke during your lifetime, and irrevocable trusts, which cannot be changed once established. Setting up a trust can be more complicated than creating a will, so it's generally advisable to seek professional guidance from an estate planning attorney. However, trusts can be particularly beneficial if you have significant assets, want to provide for a disabled family member, or have other specific estate planning goals.

Don't underestimate the importance of planning for incapacity. This involves making arrangements for someone to manage your affairs if you become unable to do so yourself due to illness or injury. In addition to a power of attorney, consider creating a living will, also known as an advance healthcare directive. This document outlines your wishes regarding medical treatment, including end-of-life care. It can specify whether you want to receive life-sustaining treatment, such as mechanical ventilation or artificial nutrition, if you are in a terminal condition or irreversible coma. A living will provides clear guidance to your healthcare providers and loved ones, ensuring that your wishes are respected. Have open and honest conversations with your family members about your healthcare preferences. This can alleviate their burden and ensure that they are making decisions that align with your values.

Tax planning is an integral part of estate planning. Understanding the estate tax laws and implementing strategies to minimize your tax liability can help preserve your assets for future generations. While federal estate taxes currently only apply to estates above a certain threshold, state estate taxes may apply to smaller estates. Work with a qualified tax advisor to explore strategies such as gifting assets during your lifetime, establishing trusts, and utilizing tax-advantaged investment accounts. Proper tax planning can significantly reduce the amount of taxes your estate owes, allowing more of your assets to pass to your beneficiaries. Estate planning doesn't have to be a one-time event; it's an ongoing process that should be reviewed and updated as your life changes. As you get married, have children, start a business, or experience other significant life events, your estate plan should be adjusted to reflect your current circumstances and goals. Make it a habit to review your estate plan at least once a year, or whenever there is a major change in your life. This ensures that your plan remains relevant and effective.

Start small and build from there. Begin by creating a simple will and designating beneficiaries for your financial accounts. As your circumstances become more complex, you can add more sophisticated estate planning tools, such as trusts and powers of attorney. The important thing is to take the first step and start planning for your future. By taking control of your estate planning, you can ensure that your assets are protected and your loved ones are taken care of, giving you peace of mind knowing that you've made responsible decisions for your future.

Finally, remember that estate planning is not just for the wealthy. Everyone can benefit from having a basic estate plan in place. Even if you don't have significant assets, you can still ensure that your wishes are respected and your loved ones are provided for.

www.ingramcontent.com/pod-product-compliance
Lightning Source LLC
LaVergne TN
LVHW022231200926
848481LV00006B/2223
* 9 7 9 8 3 4 9 5 5 1 2 9 1 *